Contents

Prefatory note

Works are referred to by outline number, cross-referenced in the Select Bibliography; for sequential references on the same page, the number will not be repeated. The edition of *Dominique* used is one of the most readily available (10), edited by Philippe Dufour, published in the Livre de Poche 'Classiques de Poche' series (no. 16076; ISBN 2-253-16076-8; 2001), page references to which are given in bold typeface, e.g. (**83**). Where there is a succession of references to the same page, the first only is given. For reasons of space, my more general debt to writers on Fromentin has had to be restricted to those listed in the bibliography. No particular edition has been specified for quotations from nineteenth-century French literature, such as Constant's *Adolphe* and Sainte-Beuve's *Volupté*, that are merely intended to provide background information.

Since I have already written a great deal on Fromentin, there is inevitably a large measure of self-quotation in this volume. However, I have sought to update my approach, in the light of recent findings, and to integrate reference, where appropriate, to manuscript variants. Much of the preliminary footwork in relation to the sources of *Dominique* was carried out by the late Camille Reynaud, to whose work I should like to pay tribute, as also to that of the late Pierre Blanchon and the late Guy Sagnes, Anne-Marie Christin and James Thompson.

I heard of a Cambridge undergraduate who felt impelled to tear her copy of *Dominique* to shreds on the Bridge of Sighs. My goal is to diminish the motivation which future students may have to follow her example.

My thanks are due to several colleagues and friends for discussion of points of detail, and especially to Roger Little, whose support has been ongoing.

B.W.   Dublin, July 2002

Chapter One

Genesis and epilogue

The genesis of *Dominique*, the tale of the 'impossible' love of the eponymous hero for a married woman, can be traced back to the enduring passion inspired in Eugène Fromentin by Léocadie Béraud. Born in Mauritius in 1817, Léocadie (whose maiden name was Chessé) was a creole and was almost four years older than Fromentin. She was a childhood friend of his in the little village of Saint-Maurice—now a suburb of La Rochelle—where she spent her summers and holidays with her widowed mother. She married Émile Béraud, a tax official, only four days before Fromentin's fourteenth birthday. It is unlikely that Fromentin realised the intensity of his feelings for her until after her marriage, when she continued to see him, in public and in private. Parental alarm at their intimacy, particularly as it developed during Fromentin's gap year between school and University, led to major family interdicts. Such behaviour was well beyond the pale of acceptability. The sense of scandal was such that, to this day, Dominique is a taboo name for any of the male descendants of the Béraud family. Notwithstanding the sanctions of society, Fromentin's romantic feelings for Léocadie stimulated his creative awakening. He wrote many poems, some of which were published in the local newspaper, others he gave to Léocadie and more again he kept himself. Some of this verse relates to Léocadie's children, lullabies evoking scenes of domestic harmony. Mostly, however, it reflects the self-awareness of adolescence, expressed in hackneyed and often derivative forms.

Absence certainly did not destroy Fromentin's love for Léocadie over the first two years of his life as a law student in Paris, returning to Saint-Maurice for the summer vacations. When he set off, in November 1841, to embark on his third year of legal studies, the family mounted an all-out assault to get him to break off the relationship with Léocadie, who was said to have promised her husband that she would mend her ways. However, Fromentin defied the parental interdict in a host of covert acts, many of which bore the hallmark of cloak-and-dagger Romanticism. He connived, with his brother and with mutual friends, to smuggle letters and small gifts to Léocadie. Early in January 1841, he was caught out, when a letter, which he had sent *poste restante* to his brother, for onward transmission, was intercepted by their mother. A dreadful family row ensued. Friends and family tried to persuade Fromentin of the hopelessness of this love affair. A devoted son, he was contrite and promised to conform to the wishes of his parents. The couple were required by their respective families not to meet during the summer vacation of 1842. Indeed, Fromentin wrote to a friend, Paul Bataillard, saying: 'Les circonstances nous désunissent malgré nous. Nous aurons la vertu des âmes fidèles, la résignation' (3, p. 213). In January 1843, after all official contact had ceased between the two families, Léocadie took the first step towards reconciliation. The following month, she gave birth to her much longed-for son, her third child. Tragically, however, illness and death were soon to follow. Léocadie, suffering from what was in all likelihood breast cancer, was rushed to Paris for surgery. She died there, on 4 July 1844.

Fromentin was at Léocadie's side, when she was terminally ill in Paris. He prayed frantically, late at night, in the nearby church of the Madeleine. The extent of his anguish is clear from the daily letters which he sent to his mother. Thanks to the intervention of a childhood friend, Fromentin was able to glimpse Léocadie through a glass door. Her husband was there. Forgetting old grudges in their moment of mutual sorrow, he shook Fromentin's hand. The last rites were said and Fromentin was present, along with close members of her family, at Léocadie's death. The death of Léocadie was a bereavement from which he would never recover, a loss which was definitively to mark the end of his Romantic youth.

Grief-stricken, Fromentin talked of taking monastic vows. Gradually, however, with the help of friends, he began to reshape his life. They kept him company every evening until they realised that solitude was no longer a threat to his stability, but rather a necessary part of the healing process. He had turned from writing to painting and had already been sketching in the outskirts of Paris. Now he would seek a new consolation in nature. In August 1844, he worked in the forest of Fontainebleau, where he sought to sublimate his grief in art.

As time went on, Fromentin came to view these events in a different perspective. A note written two weeks after the death of Léocadie testifies to a vow, of which the publication of *Dominique*, almost two decades later, could be seen as a fulfilment:

> Amie, ma divine et sainte amie, je veux et vais écrire notre histoire commune, depuis le premier jour jusqu'au dernier. Et chaque fois qu'un souvenir effacé luira subitement dans ma mémoire, chaque fois qu'un mot plus tendre et plus ému jaillira de mon cœur, ce seront autant de marques pour moi que tu m'entends et que tu m'assistes. (3, p. 280)

Back in Saint-Maurice that autumn, the idea of coping with his grief by writing about it (in the first instance, to his closest friends) gained momentum. His attachment for Léocadie had such profound roots in the depths of his being that, with her death, he felt bereaved of all the luminous and serene periods of his life. On the first anniversary of Léocadie's death, Fromentin wrote to a friend, characterising all that had been most precious to him in his love for her: 'J'avais trouvé dans son affection réciproque tout ce qu'on peut attendre d'une femme, même d'une sœur, ce qui est plus rare. J'avais, ce qui est le rêve de toute ma vie, [...] j'avais obtenu d'elle l'*amitié* dans l'*amour*' (p. 377).

When passed through the prism of memory, Fromentin's love for Léocadie became more and more idealised. Her death was the turning-point of his life, marking the end of what he called his mental puberty (p. 303) and his passage into 'the real world'. He told a friend that all his memories would date from July 1844 (p. 311). It was the catalyst for his self-awareness and self-knowledge—the equivalent, for him, of Moses smiting the rock in Horeb, from which came water for the children of Israel:

> C'est le rocher de Moïse. —Une passion vraie, quoique superficielle en apparence, quand elle date de loin, a par cela même des racines profondes et des liaisons insaisissables avec tous les faits survenus depuis son origine.—Elle touche à tout, tient à tout, ne souffre aucune atteinte qui n'atteigne aussi tout le reste; —elle est le lien de nos souvenirs; elle embrasse, résume et reproduit, dans des proportions variables, toute notre existence contemporaine. (p. 318)

This quotation says it all. As a turning point, the trauma of Léocadie's premature death has the drama of a St Augustine-like conversion, but the points of reference are secular, not spiritual. Furthermore, they will not be exported from life to art as a static 'product', but rather as the 'process' whereby the author is stimulated to shape a dynamic self-portrait, fashioned from a myriad of memories and impressions, which both recapture and create anew the kaleidoscopic elements inherent in a fictional autobiography. Even as Léocadie's funeral was taking place in Saint-Maurice, Fromentin's letters to her were being burned. In the only one which still survives, Fromentin remarked that every tiny detail associated with her went to make up his 'monde imaginatif' (3, p. 102). In so far as it represents the fulfilment of Fromentin's vow, *Dominique* functions at three levels: as a love story (set in a quasi-mythical framework); as an exercise in autobiographical self-construction; and as a dynamic exploration of imaginative creativity in art.

Dominique has long been categorised as a *roman personnel*. This expression was coined by Ferdinand Brunetière, who, in 1888, defined modern lyricism as 'l'expansion de la personnalité du poète, ou comme qui dirait encore, la prise de possession de l'univers par son *Moi*' (62, p. 234). It was reformulated successively by Joachim Merlant (68) and Jean Hytier (66). Now, however, it is sliding into disuse, since the moral purpose supposedly derived from such autobiographical writing no longer has the same ring of authenticity in the more pluralist society of recent times, with its concomitant collapse of certainties and values, and since the Death of the Author was proclaimed by Roland Barthes and Michel Foucault in the 1960s. The term *roman personnel* adapts the common eighteenth-century device of embedding a confession in a frame narration. It is a *roman*, to the extent that it seeks to distance art from reality through the medium of fiction and it is *personnel*, in the sense that it focuses, not so much on external events, but rather on interior self-examination. *Atala* (1801) and *René* (1802), published by Chateaubriand as stand-alone texts, extracted from his epic treatise, *Le Génie du christianisme* (1802), served as exemplars of the *roman personnel*. Read together, they present the archetypal portrayal of the pursuit of the impossible ideal, in the French colony of Louisiana, a refuge from turbulent post-Revolutionary France, the *ancien régime* and the heyday of the aristocracy now well and truly over. The newly-developed emphasis on subjective individualism—in part a by-product of eighteenth-century *sensibilité* and of the stream of thought which ultimately gave rise to the American Declaration of Rights—established the 'moi' as the main source of creative inspiration. Chateaubriand defended the 'genius' of Christianity in terms of aesthetics, rather than theology, maintaining that this faith has been productive of greater results, in literature and the arts, than are found in pagan masterpieces. Harking back to the Medieval and the Gothic, and arguing for the 'beau idéal', or the principle of an artistic choice in nature, the work is Romantic, rather than Classical or philosophical in spirit. More particularly, it describes 'le vague des passions', a condition indissolubly linked with the evolution of Christianity, in the view of Chateaubriand: the perpetual striving after perfection gives birth to a feeling of despair, because of the very unattainability of the goal. As is clear from Chateaubriand's self-quotation in the Preface to the 1805 edition of *Atala*, the *vague* (vagueness) of these high-flown aspirations can lead to precocious cynicism: 'L'imagination est riche, abondante et merveilleuse; l'existence pauvre, sèche et désenchantée'. This disjunction was explored and developed, as has been shown by Justin O'Brien (69), in the burgeoning novel of adolescence, centring on the sixteen-year-old René, portrayed in 'le matin de la vie'. What Chateaubriand described as 'le vague des passions' was picked up, after the triumphs and tragedies of the First Empire, by Benjamin Constant, in the Preface to the second edition of his novel *Adolphe* (1816), as 'une des principales maladies morales de notre siècle': 'cette absence de force, cette analyse perpétuelle, qui place une arrière-pensée à côté de tous les sentiments, et qui par là les corrompt dès leur naissance'. This corrosive inertia, this potentially paralysing self-analysis, this gulf separating what we feel we can do from what we actually achieve, is characterised by Senancour in *Obermann* (1804) as 'la supériorité de nos facultés sur notre destinée', and labelled by Sainte-Beuve, in his Preface to the second edition of that work in 1833, as the 'mal du siècle'. By 1849, when the failure of the 1848 Revolution had filtered through the general consciousness, Sainte-Beuve, in his book *Chateaubriand et son groupe sous l'Empire*, declared this condition a thing of the past and called it 'la maladie de René'.

This, in brief outline, shows where Fromentin was coming from. Born in 1820, and thus virtually a contemporary of Baudelaire and Flaubert (both born in 1821), he began by being drawn to the German Romantics, such as Goethe (*Die Leiden des jungen Werther*, 1774), Jean-Paul Richter (*Titan*, 1800) and Novalis (*Heinrich von Ofterdingen*, 1802), whom he read in French translation. Above all, however, he was attracted by Victor Hugo, whose poem, 'Mazeppa' (in *Les Orientales*, 1829), presented the image of the Romantic artist, alienated from society, but nevertheless destined to be its ultimate saviour. Gradually, Hugo gave way to Sainte-Beuve (*Volupté*, 1834), Balzac (*Le Lys dans la vallée*, 1835-1836) and Lamartine (*Jocelyn*, 1836), as sources of inspiration. Fromentin ended by occupying a position, aptly described by Guy Sagnes as focusing on 'le romantisme de la mélancolie' (5, p. 30), or second-generation Romanticism, characterised by a robust rejection of all that was exaggerated and exhibitionist in the pioneers of the Romantic movement, though never entirely losing the vestigial traces of that first wave of enthusiastic ardour, muted by the passage of time and modified by the inevitable setbacks of experience, to become a mood of resignation and bitter-sweet nostalgia. The opening words of *Dominique* sweep away René and the whole train of pity-seekers: '«Certainement, je n'ai pas à me plaindre»' (**41**). The victim has gone. So too has the superior genius. Dominique insists that 'il ressemblait aujourd'hui à tout le monde' (**42**). First published in serialised form in the *Revue des Deux Mondes* of April-May 1862, and in book form in 1863, *Dominique* is chronologically closer to the period of Léon Cladel's *Les Martyrs ridicules* (1862), Maxime Du Camp's *Les Forces perdues* (1867) or the *raté* of Alphonse Daudet's *Le Petit Chose* (1868) than to the Romantic Superman implicit in the very name of *Obermann* (1804). 'Pudeur', a key word often applied to Fromentin, signifies not merely timidity and inhibition, but also the sheer horror of wearing one's heart on one's sleeve. Even as it is, the central confession in *Dominique* is characterised in terms of 'des épanchements trop intimes' (**269**). In reviewing, for the *Revue des Deux Mondes* of 1836, *La Confession d'un enfant du siècle* (the very title of which echoes the *mal du siècle*), Sainte-Beuve urged Musset to stop displaying his wounds in public. However, whereas Musset saw the 'immortalisation' of his confession as a warning to others, Fromentin wrote *Dominique* both as a personal expiation and a private pleasure. 'Ce qu'il y a de plus clair pour moi,' he told George Sand, 'c'est que j'ai voulu me plaire, m'émouvoir encore avec des souvenirs' (3, p. 1233).

———

Dominique is clearly not an autobiography, in the sense of Philippe Lejeune's contractual 'pacte autobiographique' (67), the terms of which require author, narrator and protagonist to be one and the same person. It has features of the *roman à clefs*, in that Madeleine is obviously inspired by Léocadie Béraud and Dominique by Fromentin. In order to develop the anti-heroic subject of his novel, the author sought to personify the tension of opposites within the personality of Dominique by creating the countervalent forces of his charming friend, Olivier d'Orsel (openly identified by Fromentin, years later, as Léon Mouliade, his old schoolfriend: 'l'*Olivier* de Dominique' [3, p. 2040]), and his stoical tutor, Augustin (an amalgam of Fromentin's teacher, Léopold Delayant, his friend Paul Bataillard—with whom he shared an apartment in Paris—and Émile Beltremieux—who, in his short life, served as a role model for Fromentin). Madeleine's sister, Julie, was inspired by Beltremieux's sister, Lilia, whose secret love for Fromentin can be related to the equally hopeless love of Julie for Olivier. Dominique's aunt, Mme Ceyssac— 'femme pieuse et [...] demi-mère' (268)—has features in common with Fromentin's mother. The country property at Saint-Maurice, acquired by Fromentin's grandfather, Antoine-Toussaint Fromentin, blended with a nearby farm at Vaugoin to become 'Les Trembles'. Saint-Maurice itself was transmuted into the village of Villeneuve. The family town house in La Rochelle was the model for Mme Ceyssac's dark and airless house in the fictional town of Ormesson (itself a blend of La Rochelle and Saintes—the home town of Fromentin's mother).

Undoubtedly, however, the principal area of overlap between life and fiction relates to Fromentin himself. Author and protagonist were born 'dans les brouillards d'octobre' (43). They both wrote bad poetry in their youth—and destroyed it: unlike Dominique, however, Fromentin wrote no book on politics. Socially, the characters were upgraded in the novel: Dominique's family name, 'de Bray', had the *particule* 'de', characteristic of aristocratic names; so also had the family name of Olivier, Madeleine and Julie, 'd'Orsel'; in the manuscript version, Dominique, on leaving

Les Trembles, was accompanied by a 'valet de chambre', called Julien, aged about fifteen or sixteen, who stayed with him all his life (4, p. 342)—a detail which the author was clearly too embarrassed to leave in the definitive text. By contrast, Fromentin came from the provincial bourgeoisie, 'vivant étroitement de ses ressources' (**98**), despite the fact that his father was a distinguished medical practitioner, who founded and developed the first purpose-built psychiatric hospital in France, in Lafond—another village, like Saint-Maurice, but closer still to La Rochelle. Politically, both families were Legitimist, that is, they were supporters of the elder Bourbon line, driven from the throne in 1830. The recollections by Mme Ceyssac's visitors of the horrors of the Revolution are given added poignancy in the manuscript version of the novel by the detail, subsequently suppressed, that their Sunday meetings took place every week, unless 21 January happened to fall on a Sunday (4, p. 348): 21 January was the day commemorated until quite recently, in Royalist circles, as the anniversary of the execution of Louis XVI. La Rochelle, besieged in 1573 and 1627-1628 as a Huguenot stronghold, had an evening curfew (**98**) and, in the nineteenth century, when it was eclipsed as a trading port by Marseille and Le Havre, the town was characterised by the somewhat closed mentality suggested by Fromentin's twin terms of 'ennui' and 'lassitude'. 'Dominique', we read, 'avait assez peu de goût pour la mer' (**63**), mirroring the fact that Fromentin never crossed over to the neighbouring Île de Ré (now linked to the mainland by a bridge) until after he had completed his one and only novel, that is to say until he was aged forty-two. Both author and protagonist had a deep sense of roots: 'je m'enracinais, sans m'en apercevoir' (**80**), says Dominique, a feeling shared by Fromentin, despite the fact that, at times, he found La Rochelle—as opposed to Saint-Maurice—claustrophobic. In 1837, at the Collège of La Rochelle, later named after him, Fromentin came first in the *classe de rhétorique* and had the anguishing experience of having Léocadie Béraud present at the prizegiving when he had yet another year to do at school—a clear forerunner of the analogous scene in the novel.

However, the points of divergence between fiction and reality are very telling. Firstly, Dominique is portrayed as *sans famille*: 'seul de ma race, seul de mon rang' (**79**), whereas Fromentin had a constantly tension-ridden relationship with his parents, alternating between devotion and outright resistance. He and his elder brother Charles were given all the benefits of a good education and a comfortable home. However, when the younger son balked at becoming a lawyer (the only real alternative in those days to being a doctor, as his brother was destined to be), the father consistently resisted all pleas by Fromentin to be allowed to make a career as an artist. Not only was every concession grudgingly granted, but, when, in 1843, Fromentin at last obtained his father's permission to take painting lessons, this was conditional on his father choosing the teacher: the choice, predictably enough, was an arch-conservative. The situation was further complicated by the fact that Dr Fromentin was himself a good amateur painter and failed to see why his younger son could not have a secure income from a profession and do as he did—paint as a hobby. In fairness to the father, his prediction that Fromentin would find it difficult to earn a living as an artist turned out to be true: he was always strapped financially and, even when he had made a name for himself and was established as one of the prominent Orientalist painters of his day, he still had to churn out potboilers. The father, too, made the point that his son's rhetorical skills with language were such as to enable him to be a highly eloquent lawyer—a talent which was not wasted, given Fromentin's literary achievements. Although Dr Fromentin ended, years later, by rejoicing in his younger son's eventual fame and fortune, he was heard frequently to remark on what a fine career he could have had as a lawyer. Nor did Fromentin feel particularly close, as the years went on, to his brother Charles, whose good nature in youth later translated into an enervating lack of ambition and subsequently hypochondria. His mother was the family member to whom Fromentin felt closest: artistic, quiet, sensitive and prone to tears, she was nevertheless narrowly pious and subtly possessive. The fact that Fromentin wipes out all family connections for most of the protagonists in his novel must surely indicate a desire to hide and to repress, as well as an understandable respect for privacy and discretion. Dominique's mother died soon after he was born and his father died a few years later—Dominique emphasises this point still further with the comment: 'sa mort remonte pour moi bien au-delà de son décès réel' (**77**). Olivier is also *sans famille* (**118**) and lives with his uncle, M. d'Orsel, and his two cousins, Madeleine and Julie. Augustin, for his part, was *seul*, through illegitimacy (**221**). It is true, of course, that such isolation was in the literary tradition of the *roman personnel*: the birth of René, for example, cost his mother her life. In the manuscript version of

Dominique, the protagonist was born 'pendant une nuit de furieuse tempête' (4, p. 326); but, probably for aesthetic reasons, Fromentin decided not to clutter his fictional self-representation with any such unnecessary extraneous elements. The family played too central a role in his life, however, both in his devotion to it and in his resistance of it, for there not to be Freudian undertones in his systematic exclusion of such major forces in his inner, personal being.

Secondly, Dominique withdraws to a rural backwater, becomes a gentleman farmer and mayor of his *commune*, whereas Fromentin made three visits to Algeria and had a successful career as a painter in Paris, albeit very attached to his roots in La Rochelle. The one point of tangential overlap in the novel is the scene where Dominique goes to the annual exhibition of painting, known as the *Salon*, and there communes with the portrait of Madeleine. Dominique explains that he is 'très ignorant' in relation to painting, 'un art dont j'avais l'instinct sans nulle culture' (**248**)—possibly a decoy to throw the reader off the scent, or a veiled allusion to the fact that he always resented his lack of formal education in painting, due to the consistent opposition of his father at the crucial time. Like Dominique, Fromentin married someone other than his first love: Marie, the niece of his lifelong friend Armand Du Mesnil, and brought up by her uncle and grandmother, who gave Fromentin a home from home in Paris. Far from being a *coup de foudre*, this relationship was one of long maturation, characterised by the 'quasi-fraternité' (**231**) in which Olivier and Julie were brought up and which, though a virtue of outstanding merit as far as Fromentin was concerned, was anathema to Olivier. Fromentin had a daughter and lived to see his granddaughter. He was a devoted family man, as opposed to the characters in his novel, who all end up 'sans famille' (**202**), with the exception of Augustin (**219**).

Thirdly, unlike Léocadie, Madeleine does not die prematurely, but goes on living and gradually fades into a memory for Dominique. Life, in this instance, is more dramatic than fiction. Indeed, over a decade after Fromentin had immortalised his love of Léocadie in the fictional evocation of Madeleine, he relived the entire adventure—platonically this time—from 1873 to 1875, in the beautifully-crafted and voluminous letters which he wrote to Hortense Howland, an Egeria of the Third Republic, who was estranged from her husband and who was later to become part of the young Proust's circle of friends. The love of 'imbroglios' and 'situations scabreuses' (**233**), which Olivier detected in Dominique, and which titillated Fromentin in his youthful, covert communications with Léocadie, was replicated in this secret one-way correspondence (Hortense Howland replied cryptically by coded messages inserted in the personal columns of *Le Figaro*), until one day, a letter, which he had posted in Saint-Maurice, fell out of the letter box as the collection was being lifted, was salvaged from the mud and returned to the house, where it was found by his wife. Thereafter, Fromentin continued to write to Hortense Howland, though never again with the lyrical outpourings of the earlier letters which constitute a *réécriture* of *Dominique*. To begin with, he sought to heal her troubled soul, much as, in the novel, Madeleine tried to 'cure' Dominique of his love for her. Gradually, Hortense Howland became so much a creation of Fromentin's imagination that he saw her in terms of his fictional heroine, as a figure in white, with eyes of haunting fascination. Where Dominique communed with a picture of his loved one, Fromentin painted the portrait of Hortense Howland, seeking to do so without wielding 'un pinceau trop tendre' (3, p. 1761). Fromentin loved her like an ideal being, belonging to 'un autre monde' (p. 1780), a dreamlike creature, coterminous with his aesthetic aspirations (p. 1749). Throughout, he addressed her in the 'vous' form. He singled out her eyes and hands, sometimes suggesting that his thoughts were sensuous, but always acknowledging that, for him, she represented an impossible love, an absurd illusion. 'Vous êtes le roman', he wrote to her, 'le secret, le péché, la faute exquise de ma vie intérieure et réservée' (p. 1970). Fromentin's feelings for Hortense Howland had all the pathos of the nostalgia of youth, on the part of an older man enamoured of a younger woman. In a way unprecedented in his earlier correspondence, he established a parallel between his own personality and that of his eponymous hero. 'Pour mon éternel malheur', he wrote to her in 1873, 'le Dominique que je porte en moi, s'est examiné par hasard dans ses contrastes avec vous, et s'est jugé' (p. 1769). The disjunction between lover and the object of love, which had characterised his passion for Léocadie, was transmuted first into the unfulfilled love of Dominique for Madeleine and then into the idolisation of Hortense Howland. From Saint-Maurice he wrote to her, saying: 'Je vais saluer la grande mer, et lui dire votre nom tout bas. Dominique faisait cela jadis, dans ses voyages.—Il criait, sur les grèves, le nom de M...'. The identity of Hortense Howland seemed to blend with that of Madeleine:

> Maintenant M... dort ici même pour l'Éternité, dans un petit coin de cimetière de village. —On l'y a rapportée jeune, belle, amoureuse encore et morte. —Il y a de cela combien d'années. Dominique n'a pas oublié, mais il s'est consolé. Il aime encore, de même, avec plus de profondeur. Que de choses il ignorait, qu'il sait aujourd'hui. Il a vécu. Il a commis quelques fautes, pas mal de fautes; il a vieilli. Toujours il souffrait de n'être plus jeune; il n'a pourtant jamais désespéré d'aimer encore. —Il a fui quelques rencontres; —le hasard l'a conduit; —et voilà qu'il aime l'impossible aussi passionnément qu'il a jamais aimé. (3, p. 1789)

This epilogue illuminates the genesis of *Dominique*, by highlighting not merely the permanence of the inspiration of Fromentin's love for Léocadie, but also the way he was constantly reshaping his memory of it and merging the lived and the fictional versions to inspire still further elements of lived reality. Fromentin channelled his passion for Hortense Howland into the creative forces of his work. '*Aimer, créer*, c'est tout un' (p. 1844), he wrote to her, an observation which provides both a clue and a confirmation of the close parallel between love, self-representation and artistic creativity in *Dominique*. Words create rather than reflect.

———

The reflection of the Self in the words of the Other was one of the prime motivating forces among readers in the nineteenth century, the period described by the historian Alain Corbin as the century of confession (63, p. 503). The autobiographical tradition was inaugurated by Rousseau's 1782 *Confessions* and developed into what Fromentin's friend Beltremieux called '*livres-miroirs*' (3, p. 157), in which the reader could watch himself while contemplating others. These are not autobiographies, in that the identity of the protagonist is different from that of the author or the narrator. Often they are eponymous novels, in which, through invention as well as recollection, form and coherence are brought to a lived experience. They may serve a therapeutic function by enabling their authors to interpret the events of the past quite differently from the way in which they were originally perceived. Paradoxically, as observed by Amaury, the protagonist in Sainte-Beuve's novel, *Volupté*:

> Plus les choses écrites retracent avec fidélité un fait réel, un cas individuel de la vie, et plus elles ont chance par là-même de ressembler à mille autre faits presque pareils que recèlent les humaines existences.

The tradition of the *livres-miroirs* was, in many ways, a collective one, rather like that of the folk song, in which a template, so to speak, is handed down from generation to generation, with each interpreter adding his or her own individuality in the shape of grace notes, trills, or melodic variation. One could pour one's soul out to it, under the cover of anonymity, while at the same time seeing one's own reflection in the experience of the Other. Fromentin's friend, Paul Bataillard, remarked that, in their youth, their circle of friends were 'les derniers fils des Werther, des René, des Adolphe, des Obermann, des Amaury, auxquels on peut ajouter le Rousseau des *Confessions*' (13, p. 331). This manner of reading, motivated by both empathy and self-contemplation in convergent mirrors (proscribed by Augustin [**131**]), is crucial to an understanding of the genesis of *Dominique*, in terms of the tradition of which it was born, the impulse from which it stemmed and the readership which it addressed. 'Tu t'y contemples à ton aise', wrote Émile Beltremieux, on hearing of Fromentin's enthusiasm for Rousseau (most probably the *Rêveries du promeneur solitaire*, since he spoke of the 'panthéisme involontaire de Jean-Jacques'): 'C'est comme cela souvent qu'on aime lire; et c'est une des manières les moins inutiles peut-être' (3, p. 157). 'J'ai retrouvé mon histoire dans les livres des autres' (**183**), remarks Dominique. Significantly, however, at a point in the novel when he is trying to cut out emotional intelligence, he will note: 'Me reconnaître dans des livres émouvants, ce n'était pas la peine au moment même où je me fuyais' (**243**).

Fromentin's novel is, thus, grounded in literary artifice, as well as in lived reality: in Goethe's *Werther* (**126**), in Lamartine's 'Le Lac' (**183**) and in Virgil's *Aeneid* (**213**); in the sonnet 'Mon cœur a son secret, mon âme a son mystère', by Félix d'Arvers (**160**), in George Sand's *Mauprat* (**259**) and in Longfellow's poem 'Excelsior' (the title of which is inscribed three times on the walls of Dominique's study (**67**) and repeated with countless exclamation marks). There were also models nearer to home: Paul Bataillard wrote a tribute to a friend of his who had died young, *Gustave Millot: Reliquiæ* (1838), presenting anticipatory analogies with *Dominique* (59); Armand Du Mesnil wrote a novel, *Valdieu* (1860), the plot of which has many parallels with that of *Dominique* (58); in that same year, the *Revue des Deux Mondes* published a short story, 'Madame de Marçay', later attributed to Anatole Prévost-Paradol, inspired by Hortense Howland and, plotwise, another potential avatar of *Dominique*.

At a deeper level, *Dominique* has its origins in Fromentin's earlier literary work. The sonnet, 'Un nuage qui passe' (1838), in which the momentary darkening of bright day by a shadowy cloud is likened to sadness seen amidst joy, heralds the symbiotic relationship between landscape and human personality which is so central to the novel. The nagging self-doubts, which bedevelled the whole of Fromentin's career, led to an early self-evaluation, which was both harsher and more penetrating than that made by many of his critics: 'je vois *joli* et pas *grand*' (3, p. 609). The inability to 'think big', to strike out and take risks, was a feature of his own personality, which Fromentin passed on to his protagonist, haunted, like himself, by fears of his own non-genius. It is not surprising, then, that he should have pondered, in an essay entitled 'À quoi servent les petits poètes' (1846), the valuable contribution made by the *poetæ minores*, acting as intermediaries between men of genius and their public: by imitation of the Masters, they achieved greater recognition for the innovations which had been put in train. Likewise, the three journeys which Fromentin made to Algeria, in 1846, 1847-1848 and 1852-1853 respectively, in pursuit of the career which he identified for himself as an Orientalist painter, when, at long last, he was given free rein by his father, inspired the composition of two travel accounts of outstandingly high quality, *Un été dans le Sahara* (1854) and *Une année dans le Sahel* (1856). Presented in a form that is part epistolary, part *journal intime*, these writings, like *Dominique*, are motivated by the desire for self-revelation through self-projection. Fromentin seems always to have felt the need to embody his *alter ego*: the military men, M. C*** and M. N***, in *Un été dans le Sahara*, perform a role analogous to that of Vandell, in *Une année dans le Sahel*, who, in his turn prefigures the doctor friend of the external narrator in *Dominique*. These are all soundly practical people. Vandell is an ethnographer and geographer, as opposed to a painter. He executes drawings which are painstakingly accurate, but which convey nothing of the overall atmosphere of the scene. However, his limitations are as obvious as those of the doctor, in *Dominique*, who, appreciated the beautiful first evening, described in the book, 'à sa manière', 'et se perdit dans des rêveries astronomiques, les seules rêveries qu'un pareil esprit se crût permises' (**50**). It is amazing, therefore, that it should be Vandell, the man with the barometer, who, in *Une année dans le Sahel*, draws the analogy between the isolation of a landlocked expanse of water in Algeria (Lake Haloula—a lake subsequently drained by the French colonists) and that of a farm beside the sea (Vaugoin) at 'S. M***', a clearly autobiographical reference to Saint-Maurice. In Fromentin's childhood, the farm at Vaugoin was situated at what seemed to him to be 'le bout du monde' (1, p. 337). It was not until he was taken there by some huntsmen that the dimensions were scaled down in his mind. That Fromentin should have switched so personal a memory from the narrator to Vandell is evidence of his desire not to put too much of his own personality in the work. It also testifies to some degree of interchangeability between the two *personæ*, a relationship reflected in such tiny details as the way in which the horses of Vandell and the narrator 'fraternisaient' and the use of the term 'observatoire' to describe the vantage point from which they executed their drawings—a term used also in Dominique to designate the point from which he viewed nature, either at Les Trembles or in the house of Mme Ceyssac (**143-4**).

Of all the antecedents of *Dominique* in the earlier writings of Fromentin, however, the most significant is the study which he made, with his friend Beltremieux, of a now-forgotten local dramatist and novelist, Gustave Drouineau, who burned out at thirty-seven years of age and was, for a time, a patient of Dr Fromentin's at the psychiatric hospital at Lafond, where Fromentin sketched him. The 'manuscrit vert', in Drouineau's novel of that name, represents the visible conscience of the hero, Emmanuel: it is the place where he consigns his inner thoughts, the depository of his introspective self-awareness. *Le Manuscrit vert* (1832) is a sublimation in art of the tragic human experience of Drouineau, whose wife died of consumption only three years after they were married. Two years before the death of the woman whom Fromentin loved, he was taking notes of how Drouineau would make pious pilgrimages to his wife's grave and planned to write the story of their love. Similarly anticipatory of *Dominique* is the rejection of suicide as a solution. It is deemed by Fromentin to be 'le dernier argument des hommes faibles', the act of a '«déserteur»' (2, p. 27).

Fromentin goes further and reflects in general on the relationship between art and reality, and on the distinction to be made between 'des œuvres *personnelles*' and 'des œuvres *impersonnelles*' (p. 103). He defines an 'impersonal' work as one in which the author treats of 'événements réels ou fictifs tout à fait étrangers à lui-même, à sa vie morale, domestique ou sociale'. By contrast, the subjective inspiration of a 'personal' work can manifest itself in three ways.

Firstly, it can be confessional, as shown by many examples ranging from St Augustine to Alfred de Musset. Here, the author gives a direct self-portrayal, resulting in a portrait which can vary between being flattering and being disfigured, 'rarement sincère,—quelquefois minutieux et hardi jusqu'à l'indécence'. Fromentin comments caustically on how 'chacun croit devoir faire ses confessions avec une audace singulière d'analyse ou de scandale' (pp. 63-4). This is not how he considers one's private life should be expressed, details which he describes, in relation to Drouineau, as being 'trop intimes pour avoir pu trouver place ouvertement dans ses romans, —trop précieux pour être jetés à l'oubli' (p. 87).

The indirect confession is the clue to the second category of 'personal' works, in Fromentin's definition and, incidentally, the formal model for *Dominique* itself. In the indirect confession, the reader can discover, 'sous le masque de certains personnages, ou sous la fiction du conte, la physionomie morale, et les faits que l'auteur a par discrétion, par pudeur, ou par faux orgueil hésité à mettre à découvert' (p. 103). Paradoxically, distance from the lived experience can make it easier to capture and to convey to others the essence of that experience. The novelist should therefore, according to Fromentin, attempt to present the maximum of objective reality through the prism of the most personal of visions. To this he attributes the success of *Werther*, *René* or George Sand's *Lélia*, where 'la fiction se mêle au vrai, —l'idéal à la réalité' (p. 104). This blend can also accommodate the wish-fulfilment of the authors, since it enables them to bestow on their heroes 'des biens qu'ils n'ont pas, mais qu'ils attendent, des honneurs qu'ils convoitent'. Just as Fromentin himself would later do in *Dominique*, they can upgrade the social position of their fictional characters and have them accomplish 'ce pèlerinage indéfini qu'eux-mêmes ont fait déjà dans le monde irréalisé des chimères'. '«*On se dédommage ainsi*»,' observes Fromentin revealingly, '«*du bonheur qui manque*»' (2, p. 29).

The third category of 'personal' works seems to emerge more by accident than by design, in that it encompasses works in which the writer does not intend to make his presence felt, but whose creative imagination is so poor that he is incapable of imagining a character other than his own. He is like a puppeteer: '«*jamais on n'oublie qu'il est là derrière la scène soufflant et faisant mouvoir les fils de l'action*»' (2, p. 29). He intervenes—without irony—to comment on the narration, or to emphasise the moral to be drawn from it. Sadly, Drouineau falls into this category, with the result that his work, *Ernest*, ceases to be a personal novel, and moves over instead to the realm of social art.

In parallel with these distinctions, Fromentin goes on to analyse what may be said to differentiate 'les héros *actifs des héros passifs*' (p. 107). 'Active' heroes are generally to be found in plays and in novels of adventure, where human dynamism can manifest itself in external action. 'Passive' heroes are either passive by nature, like Résignée in Drouineau's novel of that name (1833), and become a pawn in the game, or, more interestingly, they are primarily concerned with their inner lives, rather than with external reality. This latter type of 'passive' hero is more suited to the analytical novel, comments Fromentin, rightly putting his finger on the danger whereby these 'passive' characters may be made to embody all kinds of abstract ideas: 'amour, haine, ambition, désespoir'. The examples he gives are 'René—Werther—Manfred—Amaury—et surtout Obermann'.

Fromentin's position on many of these points would change and develop over the years. However, from this early study on Drouineau, he had already focused on two issues which would be of central importance in relation to *Dominique*: the delicate balance between the subjective and the objective in art; and the differing tensions between the static and the dynamic in self-representation.

Chapter Two

Narrative

Fromentin had, since 18 July 1844, vowed to write the story of his love for Léocadie Béraud, but he needed to distance himself from it before he could give it form. Plot and narration did not come easily to him. 'Moi', he admitted to George Sand, 'je n'ai aucune idée de la tenue, de la logique et des vraies conditions d'équilibre d'un livre construit' (3, p. 1239). Painting had not prepared him for the linearity of narrative. Spatial representation could not take account of the layers of time involved in the parallelism between past and present, between Self and Other, which had haunted him all his life. Already, in March 1848, he acknowledged that, if ever he were to give expression to his memories, they would take on 'la forme littéraire' (p. 717). However, when he came to write the Haoûa episode in *Une année dans le Sahel*, the only dramatic incident to be found in his travel accounts, he experienced great difficulty and had to seek the help of his trusted friend Armand Du Mesnil. Nervously, in his dedication of *Dominique* to George Sand, Fromentin sought to excuse himself for 'toutes les inexpériences qui peuvent trahir une œuvre d'essai'. The text is introduced, self-deprecatingly, as a 'récit très simple et trop peu romanesque' (41).

There are two narrators: the external narrator, who introduces the reader to Dominique, the internal narrator. The external narrator is thus supposed to present the written version of an oral confidence, which, in its turn, was the verbalisation of the 'mémoires chiffrés' (76) on the walls of Dominique's study. The *récit*, told by Dominique, covers the events of some fifteen years. Started at about noon, one wet afternoon in early October, it took only a few hours to tell, and ended as daylight failed and darkness crept into the study. The external narrator, whose meeting with Olivier had precipitated the confession, then meets Augustin, with whose exemplary name the double narration closes. To keep up this 'fiction', Maija Lehtonen has calculated that Dominique addresses the external narrator sixty-five times in the course of telling his tale (37, p. 80). However, this specular strategy, whereby Fromentin hoped to set up a critical distance from the protagonist, is not applied with equal rigour at the start and finish of the tale. 'L'image extérieure et l'image intérieure,' we are told, 'pâlissaient [...] en même temps' (**270**). If the external narrator was at first in doubt as to the final resolution of the conflicts within Dominique, wondering to what extent self-proclaimed sincerity might conceal a rationalisation of failure, such hesitations are inexplicably removed at the end of the *récit*. And this, allegedly, before the external narrator wrote up his introduction, with its initial sense of detachment from the events to be recounted. In truth, the final merging of the 'image extérieure' and the 'image intérieure' points to the fact that the two narrators are not genuinely autonomous. Their mode of self-expression is stylistically identical, to such an extent that the *récit* bears virtually no trace of its origin as an oral text and is linked seamlessly with the external narration which introduces and concludes it. The reader is never told the name of the external narrator, who, like Dominique, is a keen huntsman. Indeed, they meet in the course of a day's shooting, when the external narrator was invited to the village of Villeneuve by a doctor friend of his, whose role, as we have seen, is similar to that of Vandell in *Une année dans le Sahel*. Their hunt takes them over the same terrain, with but a few hundred metres (**44**) between them. They take aim at the same partridge, which Dominique shoots and graciously gives to the external narrator, apologising for taking his shot in the interests of preventing the loss of such a fine bird. Later, when invited to Les Trembles, the external narrator sleeps in the room which had been Dominique's as a boy and hears the same wind and the same booming sound of the waves as those which Dominique would have known. In all respects, the separate identity of the external narrator is more rhetorical than real. To adopt the excellent expression of Robert Lethbridge, he functions as 'an unquestioning mirror for Dominique's images of himself' (38, p. 49).

The plot is based on the age-old theme of impossible love. An unfinished manuscript variant of the theatre scene gives the overall scenario as a *mise en abyme*, that is, as a thematic reflection within the text:

> —Au théâtre, comme dans les romans, qu'on y chante ou qu'on y
> déclame, que ce soit en prose ou en vers, en actions, en couplets, que
> le sujet soit triste ou gai, —au fond le thème unique, invariable c'est un
> homme qui aime une femme. Il la désire, il la poursuit, il l'obtient de
> force ou de gré, il la séduit, la captive, l'enlève, l'achète, se la fait
> donner; si la femme est libre cela finit par un mariage, sinon ce sont des
> catastrophes où la vie de trois personnes se trouve aussitôt engagée.
> Alors l'action devient d'autant plus pressante, le nœud plus étroit,
> l'intérêt plus vif, que l'humeur de la femme vaut davantage, que celui
> du mari court plus de risque et que le succès de la querelle est plus
> douteux. En pareil cas il y a presque toujours quelqu'un qui meurt.
> Beaucoup voudraient que ce fût le mari. Le plus souvent c'est un des
> deux coupables [...]. (4, pp. 464-5)

Impossibility is at the core of Dominique's anguished realisation:
'«J'aime une femme mariée!»' (**144**). Fromentin altered the age difference
between Dominique and Madeleine from almost four years in reality,
between himself and Léocadie, to 'deux ans à peu près' (3, p. 349), in the
manuscript version, and 'un an à peu près' (**100**), in the definitive text.
Whatever it amounted to, however, the age gap was key. Dominique was
acutely conscious of the 'distance énorme qui séparait une fille de dix-huit
ans à peu près d'un écolier de dix-sept ans' (**124**). 'Le hasard', Olivier said
to Dominique, 't'avait fait naître [...] six ou huit ans trop tard' (**163**). So,
the 'amour impossible' became 'un amour coupable' (**157**) and, as such,
was doomed. Its very impossibility seemed to galvanise it, to an extent not
expressed as lucidly by Fromentin as by Mme de La Fayette, in her
masterful portrayal of the renunciation by the princesse de Clèves of the
duc de Nemours, whom she loved dearly and whom, upon the death of
her husband, the social *bienséances* would have allowed her to marry.
Anticipating that, despite his protestations, the duc de Nemours would
soon be unfaithful to her and knowing that she could not bear that, she
declines his offer, convinced that it would not be long until he would find
another flame. 'Je crois même', she adds sagaciously, 'que les obstacles
ont fait votre constance'. Some of these same elements are traced
carefully by Fromentin in his variation on this age-old theme: the 'devoir'
in relation to the married man's position in society—'les arguments des
maris menacés dans leur honneur, ce qui est déjà grave, et dans leur
bonheur, ce qui est beaucoup plus sérieux' (**163**); and the *repos*, or peace
of mind, which is of primordial importance for the princesse de Clèves
and which Dominique optimistically envisions for Madeleine, long after

they have parted, as he thinks of her 'dans des conditions de sécurité, de bonheur et d'oubli' (**77**). Having read the final instalment in the *Revue des Deux Mondes*, George Sand maintained that Fromentin needed to add a few further pages between the last farewell of Madeleine and the marriage of Dominique. She felt so strongly on the subject that she advocated the inclusion of new material, the effect of which would have been to show the exasperation of the hero after parting with Madeleine, tantalised at having thrown away a unique opportunity, and at having acted foolishly in not acting masterfully. George Sand invited Fromentin to spend a few days in her home at Nohant, so that together they might review these and other possible changes. He went, but, in the upshot, made only a few tiny alterations to his text. Sainte-Beuve, perhaps the subtlest of Fromentin's readers, was equally perplexed by the denouement: 'Qu'avait-il à faire', he said of Dominique, 'de souffler pendant des années le feu, pour se dérober et s'enfuir au moment où il voit la flamme?' (**51**, p. 147). Where the outcome of Mme de La Fayette's novel contains a mature assessment of the complex factors weighed up by the princesse de Clèves in reaching her decision, Fromentin's novel leaves a niggling doubt as to whether Dominique might not have been found lacking in sufficient courage to address the situation, living to regret it, surreptitiously, for the rest of his life.

The impossibility of attaining the ideal is reflected throughout the plot. Dominique tries to argue that he is more like Olivier than Madeleine realises: they both pursue a goal which is 'impossible à saisir, ou chimérique, ou défendu' (**202**). The marriage, which Madeleine would have liked to arrange between Dominique and Julie, involved 'plus d'un obstacle' (**227**): when she realises that this cannot happen, she has to face the loss of 'des combinaisons chimériques' (**228**). The unrequited love of Julie for Olivier acts as a pendant to the main love story: she is also doomed to the non-fulfilment of her desires, but again, like Dominique, refuses to succumb to a Romantic catastrophe. This great wall of impossibility is metaphorised as a precipice (**165**). When Madeleine undertakes to try to cure Dominique of his love for her, she conquers the vertigo normally associated with being at the 'point le plus escarpé' (**213**) of a dangerous mission and manages to remain steady, as she maintains her position 'au bord de l'abîme'—the figurative counterpart of the scene at the lighthouse, when the whole tower seems to sway in the wind and only a 'légère balustrade' (**180**) offers protection from the 'abîme' below.

There are two subplots: one focusing on Paris, and the other on the countryside. As in the novels of Balzac, Paris is presented in contradistinction to the provinces, as 'une inévitable antithèse' (**52**). Despite determined efforts at regionalisation, it is still true today that the summit of every career in France involves location in Paris. Still more so was this the case in the nineteenth century, when it was undoubtedly 'le plus grand des théâtres' (**128**). For the struggling and hard-working Augustin, this was clearly the place where he would fulfil his ambitions (**168**). He started modestly in the Latin Quarter, 'consacré par quatre ou cinq siècles d'héroïsmes' (**133**), and flourished in this great hive of intellectual activity (**157**). Eighteen months after he had settled in Paris, Augustin wrote to his former pupil, Dominique, singing the praises of his new life. The motto of the capital city, *Fluctuat nec mergitur*, is rendered by him in the phrase: 'On y flotte et l'on ne s'y noie pas' (**130**). Madeleine, however, did not make the transplantation so easily, despite the fact that she looked forward to 'ce grand Paris' (**140**). Olivier had been in Paris before finishing off his school career in Ormesson, which gave him a 'grande supériorité' (**101**) over his peers. Having left the capital, he felt like Ovid banished to Thrace from the Rome of Augustus (**102**). Dominique too was reminded of Ovid, regretting, by contrast with Olivier, his exile to Ormesson... from Villeneuve (**103**).

The downside of Paris was its anonymity. Anne-Marie Christin has observed how, unlike the fictitious town of Ormesson, Paris is not given a single street name in the novel (8, p. 308). Dominique arrived there by night and his first impressions were decidedly negative. He was struck by 'cette fourmilière de gens inconnus qui passaient vite' (**154**). He never really settled , living there 'comme dans une hôtellerie' (**158**). In common with Balzac's picture of life in the capital, there was 'ce terrible frottement de la vie parisienne', but now, a generation later, there was the rise of industry and smoky factories (**161**). After Augustin got married, he and his wife had their first home in a nondescript suburb (identified in one of the manuscript plans as Saint-Cloud or Saint-Germain [4, p. 304]): when

Dominique visited them, Paris appeared in the distance as 'la ville entassée et fumeuse' (223). His final assessment is unsurprising: 'On disparaît si commodément dans ce grand Paris, qu'un homme aurait le temps de faire le tour de la terre avant qu'on se fût aperçu de son départ' (211).

The second subplot extols the values of the countryside. The image of the countryside is presented, in *Dominique*, as a microcosm of the universe. The burgeoning of springtime in Ormesson focuses on beauty in tiny detail, the 'insectes nouveau-nés que le vent balançait comme des atomes de lumière à la pointe des grandes herbes' (106), a loveliness reserved for those with eyes to see—in contrast to the seminarists in their black cassocks, their noses stuck in their breviaries, absent-mindedly picking the hawthorn blossoms and squeezing them in their hands.

As Roland Barthes has pointed out, the Countryside is presented by Fromentin in opposition to the City, seen as a symbol of power, worldliness and noise. By contrast, the Countryside constitutes 'un espace intelligible, où la vie peut se lire sous forme d'un destin' (16, p. 159). *Dominique* opens with the autumn of regrets. It ends with the ploughing of the soil, where seeds will be sown and time will go on, calmly and repetitively. There is a monumental quality in the 'grand geste sempiternel du semeur' (56), an image reminiscent of Fromentin's own peasant painting (dating from 1850-1851, before he dedicated himself exclusively to Orientalism) and close to that of the most celebrated of the Barbizon artists, Jean-François Millet, whose painting *Un semeur* (1850) captured this sense of the moral dignity in a worker whose face has been generalised as his task is universalised. Both Fromentin and Millet portray toiling figures as heroes and heroines, quietly fulfilling the tasks which their fate has called upon them to accomplish. Millet's works embody a profoundly conservative morality, derived from premodern society, but secularised to provide radical lessons for his contemporaries. There is some overlap here with Fromentin, who, however, is more concerned with a semi-Utopian countryside as a haven of withdrawal and personal meditation. Nature, for Dominique, is a refuge, metaphorised in the image of a wounded animal in his lair (268; 273).

———

All of which brings us to the outcome. The lovers go their separate ways. There are no dramatics. There is no suicide. However, what was announced by Dominique as a 'dénouement bourgeois' (**76**) is presented by the external narrator, at the end of the *récit*, as 'une conclusion si noble, si légitime et si évidente' (**273**). What has happened here? And what is the significance of the way in which the external narrator has been won over to Dominique's point of view?

The first element to bear in mind, in relation to the outcome, is that it involves a double withdrawal on the part of Dominique: a withdrawal from Madeleine and a withdrawal from a career in Paris. The motivation for the second of these predates that of the first. The decision to seek refuge in Les Trembles can be traced back to the night of Madeleine's wedding, when the image of Villeneuve came to Dominique, in total recall: 'je me jetai dans je ne sais quel espoir aussi chimérique que tous les autres de retraite absolue dans ma maison des Trembles' (**145**). In other words, before the relationship with Madeleine developed, and before he left for Paris, Dominique was already preparing a back-up position in the event of failure ('Le cœur est si lâche'), based on an already deeply-rooted symbiosis with nature ('il a si grand besoin de repos'). The problem is, as the external narrator admits, that the two parts of Dominique's life do not hang well together: he had 'un passé qui ne s'accordait pas très bien avec sa vie présente' (**42-3**). This difficulty was picked up almost immediately by George Sand. 'Il manque quelque chose entre le désespoir et le bonheur retrouvé' (3, p. 1238), she observed, a view echoed by many subsequent critics, including Marcel Cressot, who complained: 'Nous ne saisissons pas la raison de la retraite de Dominique aux Trembles' (20, p. 215). The dream of withdrawal was articulated by Fromentin, in his own life, as early as December 1844, some five months after the tragic death of Léocadie. The production of Armand Du Mesnil's play *Génio* at the Odéon had been postponed and there were ongoing concerns for the health of Émile Beltremieux, a consumptive. By way of consolation, Fromentin wrote to Du Mesnil, saying:

> Nous retrouverons Émile, s'il est encore de ce monde; à nous trois, nous réaliserons peut-être en petit des projets échoués sur un plus grand théâtre. —Nous bâtirions peut-être quelque chose des débris de notre fortune littéraire et artistique. À coup sûr, nous guéririons ensemble nos communes blessures. —C'est un rêve encore sans doute. —Je le crois pourtant moins chimérique que beaucoup d'autres. [...] —Vous verriez combien la vie modérée de l'intelligence et du cœur est douce en province; —et puis nous serions à Saint-Maurice peut-être. (3, pp. 327-8)

In this one brief statement, the withdrawal of Dominique is contained in embryo. Negatively, it implies failure 'sur un plus grand théâtre'—code, as we have already seen, for Paris—and suggests more modest achievements in a smaller arena. It is a dream, but 'moins chimérique que beaucoup d'autres'—almost the very words used in the novel. Then, the positive aspect of this withdrawal is hinted at, in the ultimate ideal of retirement to the countryside of Fromentin's dreams at Saint-Maurice.

These two facets of withdrawal emerge clearly from the novel. Negatively, Dominique describes himself as 'un déserteur' (**274**). The external narrator speaks of Dominique's 'retraite' (**42**), of his 'démission de lui-même' (**43**) 'dans les effacements de sa province' (**42**). And yet, asks the external narrator, how can one who is 'épris de perfection' also be 'aussi complètement résigné dans sa défaite'? Sainte-Beuve criticised Dominique's renunciation as 'timidité naturelle', posing as a 'stoïque effort' (**51**, p. 147). In the 1960s, *Dominique* was among a series of texts distributed by mayors in France to newly-married couples. This would seem to testify to the solidity of bourgeois honour implied in Dominique's withdrawal (as highlighted by Robert de Traz [53]), rather than to the unhappy love which preceded it. Others have seen in Fromentin's novel a self-righteous glorification of life in a provincial backwater: Jacques-Émile Blanche, commenting on the fact that André Gide ranked *Dominique* among his ten favourite novels (**28**), observed that it evoked the very 'somnolence domestique rurale', against which he and Gide were rebelling (**17**, p. 102). Henri Massis dismissed Dominique's withdrawal as 'fausse sagesse' (**41**, p. 289), where natural incapacity masquerades as mature resignation. In Louis Chadourne's novel *L'Inquiète Adolescence*, the narrator defends Dominique by saying: 'Moi, je trouve très beau cet homme qui renonce et qui feint d'être heureux dans la solitude'. Whereupon his friend, Jacques Lortal, replies:

> —Le pire, c'est qu'il l'est, heureux! C'est sa punition. Moi j'aurais crevé d'ennui dans mon domaine solitaire, avec ma vertueuse épouse et mes vieux serviteurs! J'aurais plutôt volé, assassiné, que de prendre du ventre, d'avoir mon banc à l'église et de digérer, après mon repas, les souvenirs de mes dix-huit ans. C'eût été plus propre. (**19**, p. 139)

That the conclusion of *Dominique* should make good right-wing propaganda is not surprising, but even this was not enough to endear the work of Fromentin to the supporters of the 'Action française' group in general and Léon Daudet (21) in particular.

On the positive side, it must be said that, for Fromentin, withdrawal did not necessarily involve mental sclerosis. On the contrary, it implied ideally a vital and active existence within a narrow and limited framework. Previously, in *Une année dans le Sahel*, he defended the role of habit in a lively apologia, describing a way of life in which the impingement of external circumstances is reduced to a minimum, with repetition and routine even being glorified:

> Faisons comme le petit Poucet, qui sema des cailloux depuis la porte de sa maison jusqu'à la forêt: marquons nos traces par des habitudes, servons-nous-en pour allonger notre existence de toute la portée de nos souvenirs, qu'il faudrait tâcher de rendre excellents. [...] C'est le moyen de nous retrouver partout et de ne pas perdre en chemin le plus utile et le plus précieux du bagage: je veux parler du sentiment de ce que nous sommes. (1, p. 225)

The cult of withdrawal was thus, for Fromentin, rooted in place, continuity and self-awareness. Sensations and experiences, when repeated, were seen to take on a new depth, like a theme invested with fuller meaning by each different variation. In a sense, this principle is symbolised by the inscriptions on the walls of Dominique's study, some of which consist of elementary geometrical figures, repeated with one or two changes of detail, modifying the pattern without altering the basic form of the design:

> [...] la figure arrivait ainsi, et en se répétant avec des modifications nouvelles, à des significations singulières qui impliquaient le triangle ou le cercle originel, mais avec des résultats tout différents. (**66**)

If, like 'le petit Poucet' or Tom Thumb, one initially creates boundaries, these need not necessarily imply any limitation in the final results and may, on the contrary, prove most fruitful. For Fromentin, the active potentialities in a life of withdrawal were just as real as the passive elements of escapism. The problem was that, in his novel, he did not present them so overtly. The manuscript, it is true, does suggest that, in retiring to Les Trembles, Dominique was responding to 'un cri vague de conscience' (4, p. 406), an absolute value within himself, from which he could not depart in the interests of his own happiness and peace of mind.

Again, in the manuscript, Fromentin shows a very adult awareness of the concomitant elements present in the withdrawal of the hero: the fear of weakness and the realisation of possible self-deception, stemming from 'un défaut de clairvoyance,' or perhaps from 'un défaut de courage' (4, p. 327). Fromentin had no complacent convictions as to the inherent virtue of such a withdrawal, but showed it rather as the necessary fulfilment of a deep, inner urge:

> Au reste, que ce soit illusion ou impuissance, qu'importe? puisque les résultats sont pareils. J'ai d'ailleurs obéi, sans me tromper, à une partie des nécessités qui résidaient au fond de mes origines. (p. 327)

Had this complexity of approach been further developed, it might perhaps have disarmed those critics, such as George Sand, who found the subtle intangibility of the conclusion inadequate. She wrote enthusiastically to Fromentin, immediately after the first instalment, impatiently awaiting the next, but already curious to know how Dominique would arrive at his final position of wisdom. Overawed, Fromentin replied, saying that he had only sought to prove that 'le repos est un des rares bonheurs possibles; et puis encore que tout irait mieux, les hommes et les œuvres, si l'on avait la chance de se bien connaître et l'esprit de se borner' (3, pp. 1232-3).

The concept of withdrawal is closely linked to that of habit—that two-edged sword well known to French thought, from Cabanis and Maine de Biran to Félix Ravaisson and Marcel Proust. Habit, in its negative function, is the enemy of spontaneity and the acolyte of dull monotony; yet, in its more positive function, it can be construed as the means of assimilating all new impressions into the network of previous experiences and of abstracting from them all that appears to be most essential and meaningful. Ravaisson, in his study, *De l'habitude* (1838), argues that habit mediates the connections between Will and Nature: as 'un *moyen terme* mobile', it ceaselessly displaces itself and is the basis of a fundamental continuity of beings, the source of all spontaneous activity.

The negative aspects of habit are clearly outlined in *Dominique*. Habit combines with 'ennui' (**94**) to make of Mme Ceyssac's town house a prison. Indeed, she and her circle of friends, with their 'amour des choses surannées' and their 'peur des changements' (**99**), are presented as having retired from the world, along with the monarchy they steadfastly supported. Life at Les Trembles seems to be in a time warp: according to the old servant André, there have been no changes in sixty years. It is easy to see how, in such circumstances, one could get into a rut: the very image used by Dominique ('c'est comme une ancienne ornière où l'on retombe' [**81**]). 'Les choses étant demeurées les mêmes', he admits, 'je vis de même'.

Yet the 'symétrie des habitudes' (**65**) is also presented as comforting, with the cyclical return of the seasons and all the associated rituals: 'l'inévitable séduction des faits qui se répètent' (**55**). The discontinuity between Dominique's past and present, as it erupts in encounters with old Jacques, and his unwelcome reminiscences (**63**), can be accommodated into the routine of everyday life, thanks to the positive force of habit. At Les Trembles, beneath the 'habitudes normales' of Dominique's existence, Madeleine came to know the 'fond caché' (**177**) of his nature.

Dominique soon came to distinguish between days of dull monotony, which he compared to 'ces bas-fonds taris qu'on découvre dans la mer à chaque marée basse et qui sont comme la mort du mouvement' (**103**), and days of heightened sensitivity and intensification of the intellect, when he experienced both 'plénitude' and 'exaltation'. These are luminous intermissions, when he is shaken out of the rut of ordinary perception and struck with a new sense of sharpness and vitality. These moments of epiphany are close to what Flaubert, in his correspondence, described as his 'grands jours de soleil', and Baudelaire, in 'Le Goût de l'infini', as his 'heureuses journées': they capture the 'surabondance de vie', extolled by Chateaubriand in *René*. This secular form of devotional experience is one which Fromentin explored in greater depth in the manuscript of *Dominique*, in relation to his 'jours de vitalité particulière', which constituted pinnacles of human existence such that:

> [...] il en résultait je ne sais quel équilibre de facultés, quel accord absolu de sensations et de rêveries, et quel bien-être extraordinaire, qui me représentaient, en attendant des félicités plus réelles, l'idéal parfait de la vie humaine dans sa plénitude de force et d'expansion. (4, pp. 358-9)

In the manuscript, he dramatised these polarities in terms of '*«le pôle glacé»*' and '*«l'Équateur ardent»*' of his life (p. 359), a parallel reduced to the more muted image of the revolving lights of a lighthouse in the definitive text (**103**). The effect, however, is indisputably an example of the secularisation of inherited theological ideas and ways of thinking, or what M.H. Abrams describes, in *Natural Supernaturalism*, as the 'displacement from a supernatural to a natural frame of reference' (61, p. 13). It can be linked to what Fromentin described to Bataillard, in 1844, as the 'lieux culminants de la vie', from which 'on domine, on possède, on gouverne en quelque sorte d'un bout à l'autre toute sa destinée' (3, p. 318).

The positive and negative aspects of withdrawal are metaphorised in *Dominique*, the latter by the 'monotonie de mouvement assoupissante' (**223**) of the windmills near Augustin's home on the outskirts of Paris, and the former by the pleasure derived from the practical task of sawing wood with Augustin (**223**)—an anticipation of the way in which Dominique will later 'cultivate his garden', in the manner of Voltaire ('Je fertiliserai mes champs' [**275**]), though with periods of inner contemplation, both in his study and in communion with nature. Dominique ends by having 'une vie de dilettantisme agréable' (**201**). The meaning of the term *dilettante*, in this context, needs to be placed in a historical perspective. Unlike the pejorative associations with 'superficiality', which it conjures up in modern usage, *dilettante*, in the eighteenth century—and still in the nineteenth century—implied connoisseurship, literally a delight in the fine arts. In 1732, a group of British patricians, all alumni of the Grand Tour, founded the Society of Dilettanti to celebrate their shared joys in art. The term is cognate with the Italian *sprezzatura*, Castiglione's concept of the art which hides all art and which leads to a state of *grazia*, in which there is a harmonious equilibrium between spiritual and practical activity, between the ideal and the real. This balance perfectly encapsulates the withdrawal sought by Dominique to a life in which he was 'moitié paysan et moitié *dilettante*' (**80**), the more so when one recalls that, in the prefatory remarks to *Les Maîtres d'autrefois* (1876), Fromentin described himself as 'un pur *dilettante*' (1, p. 568).

Self-discovery in withdrawal functions primarily in terms of memory, which is key to the structure of *Dominique*. In one sense, remembering, in this novel, is constative: the *récit* derives from the 'reading-off' by the internal narrator of the inscriptions on the walls of his study. The inscriptions serve quite consciously as mnemonics (**68**), in an ongoing attempt to rescue the events of the past from oblivion. At the end of the pastoral idyll at Les Trembles, Dominique wills himself to remember the trace of Madeleine's footsteps on the damp earth (**186**). Similarly, as a boy at Les Trembles, he voluntarily recalled 'ce monde ailé, subtil, de visions et d'odeurs, de bruits et d'images, qui m'avait fait vivre pendant les huit autres mois de l'année' (**86**). In the manuscript version of Dominique's visit to Madeleine's bedroom, during her absence on vacation with her father and Julie, he took a pair of scissors which he found on the table and carved his initials on the woodwork of the window, together with the word '*Remember*', written in English (4, p. 369). The inscriptions on the walls of his study were, quite literally, an *aide-mémoire*, 'des scellés commémoratifs', useful for sharpening his memories, 'si mes souvenirs sur ce point n'étaient pas infaillibles' (**81**).

Yet, clearly there is more to the *récit* than merely reading off these inscriptions. The internal narrator is actively shaping and constructing an associative network of impressions, experiences which are an organic part of what he is now, both consciously and unconciously. This fusion of the real and the imaginary underlies Fromentin's concept of affective memory. Dominique, like the author of the novel, was endowed with 'je ne sais quelle mémoire spéciale assez peu sensible aux faits, mais d'une aptitude singulière à se pénétrer des impressions' (**79**), an attribute which suggests certain striking similarities with Proust. When Dominique ventured into Madeleine's bedroom during her absence, he found the memory of her presence all-pervasive. As with Proust, the total recall was instantaneous, involuntary and integral: instantaneous, in that the whole experience lasted only 'quelques minutes' (**116**); involuntary, in that the 'odeur subtile' of Madeleine came back to him, without any conscious effort on his part, as had happened earlier in relation to the sound of her voice or her habit of twisting her hair; integral, in that, through the combination of physical sensations and the distance afforded by memory, he had the revelation of a fuller perception of reality than when he was actually with Madeleine, by means of new impressions, hitherto unsuspected: 'impressions dont la nouveauté [...] paraissait exquise'. For Fromentin, as also for Proust and many other writers concerned with the affective memory, the recall of a physical sensation can open up new horizons for the imagination by playing on things absent or past, while, at the same time, the sensation itself is given a new freshness and vitality by being experienced in the present.

Examples of this phenomenon recur frequently in *Dominique*. The protagonist recalls his childhood memories of going to look for traps in a ploughed field (**79**) and remarks how strange it is that, many years afterwards, he should remember not just the actual fact itself, but also the exact weather conditions prevailing at the time, the direction of the wind, the calm of the air, the grey sky and the sails of the windmills—all peripheral sensations perceived after a long interval of time by means of the affective memory. On the night of Madeleine's wedding, the cry of a curlew has the power of carrying Dominique back to the scenes of his childhood, instantaneously, involuntarily and integrally, as with Proust: 'Avec la lucidité d'une imagination surexcitée à un point extrême, j'eus en quelques minutes la perception rapide, instantanée, de tout ce qui avait charmé ma première enfance' (**145**).

However, although the operation of the affective memory in the work of Fromentin gives rise to a deep sense of permanence, and although Dominique is in quest of his self-identity (**67**), analogous to the Proustian 'vrai moi', Fromentin does not develop as fully as Proust the conquest over time. The invasion of the past on the present is central to the Proustian discovery. For Fromentin, the point of emphasis is entirely different: so far from the past invading the present, the percipient is nearly always transported back to a moment in the past. 'Et ne vous étonnez pas', warns Dominique, 'si je divague en vous parlant de réminiscences qui ont la puissance certaine de me rajeunir au point de me rendre enfant' (**81-2**). The whole of Proust's attempt is to recreate the sense of immediacy in a recurrent impression, complete with its entire initial impact, and with time destroyed. Fromentin, on the other hand, presents his recollected impressions from a distance, simplified and strengthened by their long duration: 'Le temps les fortifie, la distance peut les prolonger indéfiniment sans les rompre' (**54**). Thus, although Fromentin's memories, like those of Proust, are sharply recalled, they are set within the framework of time and not outside it. Essentially, then, these two approaches towards the concept of affective memory, although strikingly similar in many respects, differ in that for Proust the result is the conquest over time, and for Fromentin a resigned acceptance of its passing.

———

Let us return, in conclusion, to the question posed earlier in this chapter: what is the significance of the way in which the external narrator has been won over to Dominique's point of view? Conceived of as a 'witness' (**41**), he begins by affording distance and objectivity. Gradually, however, as memory turns anterior into interior, the identities of the two narrators merge and the confession is seamlessly metamorphosed into an indulgent hearing. If the plot is triangular (the two women in Dominique's life; Dominique divided between admiration of Augustin and affection for Olivier), its structure is cyclical—emblematised in the variations on the form of the triangle and the circle in the inscriptions on the walls of Dominique's study. The protagonist is torn between his past and his present, as witness his 'double bibliothèque, l'une ancienne, l'autre entièrement moderne' (**65**). Despite his irritation when others seek to remind him of happier days (**63**), thus highlighting the rift latent in the infrastructure which he has so carefully established at Les Trembles, he withdraws to his turret study to commune with his earlier *personæ*. C.J. Greshoff (31) is surely right to see in this study a projection, not merely of Dominique's mind, but also of the novel itself. In the manuscript, Dominique ends by giving orders to André, the faithful retainer, to 'recrépir' (4, p. 477) the walls of the study where he had so carefully inscribed his graffiti, which were, in effect, his lifeline. Not to have suppressed this in the definitive text would have been to commit semiotic suicide.

Chapter Three

Characterisation

At the school prizegiving in 1837, when Fromentin came first in the *classe de rhétorique* (until recently the name of the penultimate school year in France, ahead of *philosophie*—the equivalent of the present-day *classe terminale*), he read his essay, entitled 'Apologie des lettres'. Two fellow-students read their respective essays, 'Apologie de la science' and 'Avantages de l'alliance des lettres avec la science'. It was customary, in such ceremonies, to combine thesis, antithesis and synthesis. The lesson, in terms of rhetoric, was well learned by Fromentin, for whom structure—in particular, antithesis—was central to his mode of thinking. So, when it came to developing the antiheroic subject of his novel, he was so concerned to have Dominique steer a middle course between the Scylla of the endearing Olivier and the Charybdis of the self-willed Augustin that both of these embody abstract ideas in the very way he had warned against, when discussing 'passive' characters in his study on Gustave Drouineau. The result is that, almost too obviously, Olivier's way of life is intended to symbolise the dangers inherent in Romanticism, while the edifying example of Augustin is designed to inspire ethical strength and tenacious determination.

Taking, first, the case of Olivier, Fromentin self-avowedly based him on his schoolfriend Léon Mouliade, though, in portraying Olivier's 'ennui' (**73; 234-5; 273**), he brought him into line with the *mal du siècle* and the whole tradition of frivolous, Epicurean and aristocratic youths, from Byron to Musset. Olivier, in his 'dandysme' (**72**), is 'élégant sans viser à l'être' (**101**). He is that quintessentially nineteenth-century Parisian phenomenon: a 'flâneur' (**102**). He is 'toujours partout et nulle part' and is thus endowed with a quality of mobility, which gives him something of the indefinable charm of Proust's Saint-Loup, an elusive figure, slipping in and out with the utmost delicacy and grace of movement.

By contrast with the main plot of the novel, fiction proved more dramatic than fact: Olivier attempted suicide. Incidentally, there is an element of failure, here too—reminiscent of *Le Lys dans la vallée*, where

Félix de Vandenesse's intention of throwing himelf into the River Loire is thwarted by the height of the parapet on the bridge. It is Olivier's *attempted* suicide, then, which triggers the narration of Dominique's story, whereas Mouliade had an honourable but dull career as a judge, took early retirement—from a position which Fromentin, perhaps imagining what his own career might have been like, had he complied with his father's wishes, characterised as 'une mort anticipée' (3, p. 501)—and buried himself in an isolated country property in Brittany. Olivier's letter, written from Orsel, in the definitive text, is, in the manuscript, dated 'La Meilleraye, 10 novembre 18....' (4, p. 325). La Meilleraye is a Trappist monastery in the South of Brittany and Fromentin, clearly not wanting to introduce a religious dimension into the plot at this point, suppressed this reference. Convinced that Mouliade had an 'idée fausse de la vie' (3, p. 2040), Fromentin nevertheless felt a deep sympathy towards him and spoke affectionately of his 'bonhomie' and his 'excellent cœur' (p. 531). In the novel, as well as displaying the mortal self-disgust and coldly disciplined distinction of the traditional dandy, Olivier is undeniably attractive, even though the fatal impasse of his way of life is clearly shown.

The real-life counterpart of Augustin is not so clear as that of Olivier. Of the various people whom Fromentin had in mind, the most likely model is his friend Émile Beltremieux. Dynamic and full of initiative, Beltremieux tried his hand at various forms of writing—poetry, plays and political essays in particular—and achieved a considerable success in them all. Later, like Augustin, he became the secretary of 'un homme politique éminent' (**169**), in the person of Armand Marrast. Beltremieux died of consumption at the age of twenty-nine. During his short life, he seemed to Fromentin to be a 'maître' or 'guide' (3, p. 693), a relationship which Fromentin was keen to preserve, changing Augustin's age, when he came to tutor Dominique at Les Trembles, from eighteen, in the manuscript (4, p. 330), to twenty-four—but looking thirty in the definitive text (**80**). The long hours spent in discussion in Beltremieux's study in La Rochelle—including the period when they worked together on the study of Gustave Drouineau—inspired Fromentin to write 'l'histoire de cette chambre à tout jamais vénérable' (3, p. 693). Dominique's study has its origin in this '*sanctuaire*' (p. 694). Yet, temperamentally, Augustin and Beltremieux were different. Whereas Beltremieux was an ardent idealist in search of a Utopian society, Augustin is more of the self-made man, seeking to rise within the existing order. Beltremieux's idealism embraced such distant domains as Hindu philosophy and the occult sciences, worlds not dreamt of in the more pragmatic vision of Augustin.

For Augustin, life is like a chess board ('un échiquier' [**88**]). He is stoical, his courage is unshakable (**170**). He plans his career as though he were the tactician of a military battlefield. Unlike the aristocratic Olivier, Augustin's origins are extremely modest. He belongs to those 'qui [...] partent de rien pour arriver à quelque chose' (**133**). As such, he owes something to the heritage of Rastignac and Julien Sorel, without attaining to such heights as these. At times, he seems rather too abstract and is almost insufferably right at every turn. He is shown to be not so much 'un grand homme' as 'une grande volonté' (**273**). Madeleine thinks he is the embodiment of willpower (**148**), and sees his limitations: his judgement is sound in all matters, 'en dehors des besoins du cœur'. Despite Dominique's admiration for the stamina of Augustin, he perceived, in his former tutor's way of life, wretchedly straitened circumstances which made him shudder in spite of himself (**219**). In contrast to Augustin, Olivier stands for *ennui*, although he is perhaps too precociously what he is, from the very beginning, with nothing to motivate the origins of his disillusionment and nothing to explain why he attempts suicide in later life, or indeed why then rather than at any other stage. Dominique is rather too obviously flanked by these two semi-symbolic figures. Between them there is an instinctive antipathy: they can see each other's good points, but Augustin will always scorn the frivolous aristocrat in Olivier, the dandy; Olivier respects Augustin, but thinks of him as a *parvenu*, a sweating pedant (**155**), and mocks at the vision of his honest poverty.

The remaining secondary character, locking into this system of checks and balances, is Julie, Madeleine's sister. Originally 'Pauline' (4, p. 349), she may have been called after Julie de Neuillan, the counterpart of Madeleine in Du Mesnil's novel *Valdieu*. Lilia Beltremieux, sister of Émile, is widely agreed to be the real-life counterpart of this character. Fromentin held her in the highest esteem. They drew closer immediately after the death of Émile. Lilia was an accomplished artist and later correspondence shows Fromentin giving her advice about painting. As Camille Reynaud has indicated, the friendship dates back to some of the meetings between Fromentin and Léocadie, at which Lilia, also a friend of Léocadie's, is said to have been present (45, pp. 53; 85). Lilia is also known to have been secretly in love with Fromentin herself. If Dominique is torn between two polar opposites, in the persons of Olivier and Augustin, Julie presents a reversed parallel situation to that of Dominique. At Madeleine's wedding, when he took Julie's arm, their emotions were similar (**141-2**). At high noon, in the boat scene, only Julie and Dominique were awake—at opposite ends of the vessel: she, too, was lost in reverie, watching a ship, with tall, spreading white sails getting under way, far out on the horizon (**181-2**). In the ball scene, neither of them enjoyed themselves: Julie only danced reluctantly (**190**), and Dominique refused to dance at all. Highly perceptive and increasingly more withdrawn, as she gradually realises that her love for Olivier is unrequited, Julie comes across as 'cette singulière fille clairvoyante et cachée' (**264**). She, like Dominique, has to try to come to terms with the non-realisation of her dreams. She, too, reaches only a partial reconciliation with reality and, doomed to 'de longs jours misérables' (**257**), finds consolation in nature, returning from a walk during her convalescence, 'ranimée, rien que pour avoir respiré la senteur des chênes'.

What is most significant about the major female character of the novel is how little we know about her. Originally called Marguerite (4, p. 350)— quickly changed, no doubt to avoid confusion with Fromentin's daughter, who also bore that name—the elusive personality of Madeleine appears differently before and after the idyllic stay at Les Trembles, in Chapter XI. Chapters I to VIII of *Dominique* were composed with apparent ease by Fromentin, relatively few changes or corrections encumbering the carefully written manuscript. In these, Madeleine is almost incorporeal. She is introduced in a general aura of whiteness. Her eyes seem only half-open, as though she were waking up. Her 'taille' is 'indécise' (**100**). Later, she comes alive through her 'odeur exotique' (**115**), which Dominique recalls, in her absence. Her real presence is, however, conveyed through her 'regards'. When Dominique, in the middle of his crisis of adolescence, goes on an exuberant walk and feels his ever-growing potential develop, in harmony with the burgeoning of springtime, he meets Madeleine: 'nos yeux se rencontrèrent [...] pour la première fois je venais de la regarder' (**113**). When she returned from the vacation with her father and sister, Madeleine's figure is described as having 'je ne sais quoi [...] de mieux défini'; her 'regard' was 'plus rapide'; her voice had 'je ne sais quelle plénitude nouvelle' (**123-4**). When Dominique received his prize, the first 'regard' (**150**) he met was that of Madeleine. In short, the Madeleine of the period before Les Trembles is not so much reminiscent of Léocadie Béraud as of Haoûa, the ethereal female character in the episode which Du Mesnil helped Fromentin to write in *Une année dans le Sahel*. Significantly, when revising Du Mesnil's draft, Fromentin made it less dramatic and made the woman scarcely visible. To convey her presence, the use of an impersonal verb, *olet*, was invoked, enabling the agent to be omitted altogether, thus adding to the sense of immateriality of Haoûa, in terms of the scent which she exhales. Pictorially, Haoûa is the counterpart, in Fromentin's creative imagination, of Delacroix's *Femmes d'Alger*. She represents his ideal of femininity in terms of disincarnation. Her name— although Fromentin does not allude to this—is the Arabic for 'Eve'. She is a perfume, a name—made up of many vowels, 'une impression musicale' (1, p. 217). Madeleine is 'une odeur subtile' (**116**), a singing voice— recalled by Dominique in her absence (**115**)—and, above all, 'un regard'. This disembodied beauty is the essence of the legacy of Léocadie Béraud, described by Fromentin in 1847, and again in 1875, as '*l'ombre d'une ombre*' (3, pp. 532; 2028). This is what was transmuted into *Dominique* and later into his love for Hortense Howland. It was, in short, a projection of Fromentin himself, as Anne-Marie Christin has shown with great subtlety: 'sorte de transposition féminine de ces apparences qui le troublaient et le ravissaient sans fin—ou plutôt de l'inquiétude exquise qu'il goûtait à les contempler' (8, p. 40).

By contrast, the composition of the novel after Chapter XI was more laborious. One of the manuscript plans (4, pp. 303-4) shows how Fromentin sought to relate Madeleine thematically to the novelistic tradition: a theatre scene; a bouquet of violets—a 'scène courte et violente à trouver'; an outline of the final scenes with Madeleine and of the return to Les Trembles. None of these came easily to Fromentin: the 'scène violente', born of Madeleine's jealousy on seeing a former flame of Dominique's, was 'à trouver' and was not written spontaneously. As far as Madeleine was concerned, a body did emerge from the chrysalis: at the ball, her 'tenue' was 'splendide et indiscrète' (**188**). It was inspired, however, neither by Léocadie nor by Haoûa, but by female stereotypes and literary clichés. Love as a disease needing a remedy—a theme running through literature from Chrétien de Troyes to Chaucer, Shakespeare and Goethe's *Werther*—is picked up by Musset, in *La Confession d'un enfant* *du siècle*, where, to no avail, Desgenais becomes a 'physicien' and, later, Brigitte a ministering angel. '«Guérissez-vous seulement', says Madeleine, echoing the words of her literary avatars, 'je vous y aiderai»' (**207**). She conducts her work of mercy with the enthusiasm of a conscientious physician (**213**) and is devastated when Dominique tells her: '«Vous m'avez guéri, Madeleine, je ne vous aime plus»' (**214**). After playing the role of 'consolatrice ingénieuse' (**216**), she becomes more passionate: 'un être nouveau, bizarre, incohérent, inexplicable et fugace'. During this time, she gets closer to her father and sister, who go on living with her after she has got married. Her husband, comte Alfred de Nièvres, somewhat stiff and standoffish (**193**), is presented for what he is—a member of the establishment, part of the social fabric of society which is to be maintained by strict adherence to marital vows: 'il représentait l'empire de la raison avant de personnifier celui du droit' (**137**). Madeleine's sorrow at having no children comes across clearly in the novel (**202-3**; **261-2**), a feeling reflected in Julie's grief on the death of the child whom she had been looking after in the nearby village (**255**). However, a telltale detail was dropped from the manuscript, in the scene where Madeleine invites Dominique to join her in her box at the theatre: '«Mon cher mari commence à se passer de moi»', she says (4, p. 464). The only overt expression of this loveless marriage in the novel comes in the form of an image, where Madeleine leans on her husband's arm in a show of unity, and Dominique is reminded of a statue propped up by an iron rod, without which it would topple over (**217**). After the embrace of Dominique and Madeleine, following on their ride through the woods (echoing that, not merely of *Mauprat*—an analogy inserted in the text by Fromentin in deference to George Sand—but also of Emma Bovary and Rodolphe), his face is so ravaged that he barely recognises himself in a mirror (**264**). The later Madeleine, an artificial construct, is another facet of Fromentin's self-projection. After the rupture with Madeleine, the passionate part of Dominique's personality is diminished.

———

If the secondary characters reflect aspects of the protagonist's personality, if Madeleine is essentially a self-projection of Dominique, if the turret study is a self-projection of the internal narrator's mind, if, that is, these subject doubles reveal him to himself, then it is hardly surprising that Dominique's opposing selves come across in terms of the duality of his personality: 'Il y avait deux hommes en Dominique' (**69**). The self that acts and the self that observes were caught in a stalemate, resulting in an almost incurable inertia. Dominique's mind, as an adolescent, was 'plié en deux, comme un fakir attristé qui s'examine' (**105**). From Paris, Augustin reminds him of the myth of Narcissus, as told in Ovid's *Metamorphoses*, and warns him of the threat of paralysis contained in excessive self-contemplation. Dominique is, however, cast in the mould of Narcissus, and re-enacts the archetypal drama of self-delusion in a timeless world. The figure of Narcissus, as such, is also evident in the Cherubino-like Olivier (the analogy is made by Augustin [**134**]): as with the son of Cephisus, who, in Ovid's account, 'had turned sixteen and could pass for either child or man', Olivier was haunted by the figure of Julie (his long-suffering Echo) and ended by becoming the object of his own desire, while playing with the affections of others. The confident virility of Augustin combines with the irresolute sexuality of Olivier to yield an ambiguous, hermaphroditic (Hermes + Aphrodite) model for Dominique. The very name of Dominique, like Claude, is one of the French appellations which can be given to both males and females. In this connection, the suggestion, made by both Roland Barthes (16, p. 163) and John Fleming (25, p. 124), that the name is androgynous, takes on its full significance.

The centrality of the theme of narcissistic self-contemplation is evident in Fromentin's fascination with mirrors. Already in his study on Drouineau, he had noted the threat to veracity involved in any attempt to give an account of the story of one's life, remarking on 'le plaisir que certaines gens éprouvent à essayer devant [...] une glace l'effet d'un travestissement' (2, p. 104). After the death of his uncle, following shortly on that of Léocadie, Fromentin caught a glimpse of himself in a mirror and thought that it suited him to look pale (3, p. 305). In his unfinished novella *Valentin*, the protagonist takes a candle and watches himself in a mirror with 'un amer sourire' (1, p. 874). Fromentin had retained, from his youthful readings of Jean-Paul Richter, a fascination with the idea of self-contemplation in a mirror, by candlelight and at midnight, and included such a reference in the manuscript version of his novel:

> Peut-être avez-vous entendu parler d'une singulière gageure inventée pour effrayer les enfants ou les femmes peureuses. Il s'agit d'entrer

seul, la nuit, dans une chambre inhabitée; et là, debout devant une
glace, un flambeau d'une main[*sic*], de regarder sa propre image, les
yeux grands ouverts et d'un regard intense: puis, au moment où minuit
sonne, de s'appeler à haute voix, par son nom, jusqu'à trois fois. On
prétend qu'il y a peu de gens assez courageux pour supporter une
pareille épreuve. Eh bien, cette angoisse réelle ou non peut vous faire
imaginer ce que j'éprouvais dans ce continuel tête-à-tête avec mon
image aussi devant le pâle et nocturne miroir de ma conscience. (4,
p. 362)

This variant was suppressed, but, in the perfect stasis of the boat scene,
which forms part of the pastoral idyll at Les Trembles, the sea is
represented as a 'miroir terni' (**181**), a maritime equivalent of the
sheltered pool of Narcissus. Dominique, with mixed feelings of rapture
and of torment, contemplates Madeleine asleep on the deck of the boat. In
turn fleeing her presence and transforming her into a passive mirror in
which he can see himself reflected as he would wish to be, Dominique can
never consummate his relationship with Madeleine, since to do so would
be sacrilege and would cause both of them to perish, as surely as
Narcissus had done. The narcissism of Dominique is still more marked in
the manuscript version of the novel, where his continual self-scrutiny is
described as 'cette voluptueuse et funeste manie de me regarder vivre
surtout à une [...] époque, où je n'avais pas même essayé de vivre' (4,
p. 356). Augustin warns Dominique of the dangers of surrounding himself
with 'miroirs convergents', 'pour en multiplier l'image à l'infini' (**131**),
which is precisely what he does, except that the angles between the
convergent mirrors are so minimal as to present a single image: a
composite self-portrait.

From a broader perspective, it is clear that the *roman personnel*, in
the sense of the novel of formation, hardly at all self-critical in its earlier
manifestations, is now, at the hands of Fromentin, becoming Romantically
intrigued with its own reflection. The novel is beginning to be concerned
with the process of narration. This process will gradually invade the fiction
itself, using the text narcissistically as its own mirror, until the coming of
age of the modern self-reflexive novel in Gide's *Les Faux-Monnayeurs*,
where the protagonist, Édouard, is writing a novel about a writer
composing a novel called *Les Faux-Monnayeurs*: the *locus classicus* of
the *mise en abyme*. According to the diary entry of Edmond de Goncourt
for 12 December 1876, Fromentin had confided in Du Mesnil, some

months before his death earlier that year, that he wanted to write one last book, 'un livre qui montrerait comment se fait la production dans un cerveau', adding, in an outburst of enthusiasm: '«Vois-tu, tu ne sais pas ce que j'ai là-dessus!»' (65: II, 720). In a sense, he had touched on this concept of literary creativity in *Dominique*, where he has the young hero walk through the countryside in a state of rapture, 'dans une sorte d'ivresse, rempli d'émotions extraordinaires' (**108**), and return to his room in this state of intense vigilance, responding, with his whole being, to the various sense impressions which impinge upon him, 'écoutant, voyant, sentant, étouffé par des pulsations d'une vie extraordinaire' (**109**). The sunset seems to illuminate the images around him in a new and stimulating way. The sound of a military march is carried clearly through the air; and the rhythm of the music seems to act as a basis on which his poem is constructed, like complex harmonies on a repeated ground bass: 'une sorte de mode et d'appui mélodique sur lequel involontairement je mis des paroles' (**109-10**). That night, Dominique composes feverishly, as though led involuntarily by a supernatural power and releasing, in the process of composition, the turbulent feelings which had been welling up within him and which were clamouring for expression. The work over, there then follows a period of blissful calm, of 'lassitude délicieuse' (**111**).

In the manuscript version of this same passage, Fromentin gives a more ardently Romantic account of the Muse's visitation: with outstretched arms, the poet implores her to return, but in vain. This was suppressed, presumably because its flamboyancy would have been out of keeping with the quiet tone and antiheroic subject of the novel. There is more to it, however. The Muse theory elevates to a dominant position the element of mystery in creation, the *terra incognita* of genius. Such a view, as held in its extreme form by many of the first Romantic generation, amounted to a belief in a gratuitous grace, a ghostly dictation in which the role of the artist was reduced to that of an amanuensis. This magical intervention by the Muse needs to be set against earlier attempts to account for inspiration in terms of a mechanical process,—attempts which aimed at extending to the realm of the mind the discoveries which had recently taken place in experimental science. Before the nineteenth century was far advanced, however, the psychology of invention was coming to be described in terms, neither of a machine, nor of a Muse, but as a self-generating growth. The warring extremes of conscious application and supernatural vision were gradually becoming resolved, with spontaneity being valued as a fitting recompense for hard-earned skill. Among Baudelaire and his contemporaries, the Romantic concept of divine inspiration was being combined with the Parnassian insistence on workmanship to form a conception of art which would, in time, lead to Valéry's exaltation of consciousness in the creative process. Two excised manuscript variants show how Fromentin was beginning to think along the same lines. The first of these shows Dominique's fear of cabalistic sorcery: 'cette langue étrangère à la nôtre, cabalistique faite à l'usage de certains hommes et qui crée entre eux comme une franc-maçonnerie de langage et de pensée' (4, p. 377). The second uses the analogy of a machine to describe the complex workings of the human mind, in an analysis of the relationship between conscious will-power and the unknown First Cause, or 'force première', concluding that a mere 'grain de sable' is capable of overthrowing the whole intricate mechanism:

> [...] j'assistais moi-même avec une sorte d'enthousiasme à ce prodigieux travail d'un esprit en ébullition qui fonctionne même à vide. Dans ces moments-là, le mécanisme des facultés, leur engrenage, leurs correspondances; les complicités *de l'une avec l'autre*, comment la mémoire agit, et par quels fils elle s'attache à l'imagination, la multitude et la ténuité de tous ceux qu'elle fait mouvoir à son tour; la puissance de la volonté comme levier; puis le moteur principal de ce vaste système, la force première, comment se produit-elle et où? et la parfaite et fragile union de tant de pièces si distinctes, et pourtant si bien assemblées; et le petit accident, un temps d'arrêt, le grain de sable de Pascal qui peut tout suspendre et tout briser... tant de questions, tant d'examens me faisaient oublier que cette grande machine avait besoin d'un but. Et par certains moments cela me suffisait. Mais il y en avait d'autres, où je partageais l'avis d'Olivier sur le sentiment de mon impuissance. Et ces jours-là j'étais moins heureux. (4, pp. 422-3)

This account of the creative imagination, projected by Fromentin on to the narcissistic self-awareness of Dominique, takes as its starting point physical reactions to external stimuli. By thus according primacy to the 'mécanisme des facultés', Fromentin was endowing Dominique with his own hyper-acute sensibility. From an early stage, the protagonist observed that he differed from his young companions in being able to experience 'des sensations qui toutes paraissaient leur être étrangères' (**79**). This gift led, in turn, to the complex interfusing of physical sense impressions, either among themselves or with mental states: 'leur engrenage, leurs correspondances'. Synaesthetic transpositions, in the sense of analogies between one kind of physical experience and another, are not so common in *Dominique* as those between physical experiences and their mental attributes. When Fromentin claimed that his inner moods were dependent on the fluctuations of the barometer, observing how 'ce petit instrument nous gouverne' (1, p. 252), he was hardly exaggerating. Physical sensations are evoked together with their mental connotations. The young hero, for instance, tells of the bitter-sweet reaction produced in him by the changing aspects of nature: 'tant de sensations dont j'étais traversé, délicieusement blessé dans tout mon être' (**87**). Conversely, mental states in the novel are frequently suggested by means of associated physical sensations. Madeleine's wedding, for instance, is connected in Dominique's mind with a vivid memory of the acute physical pain which he experienced at the time and which lingered on, 'comme la trace d'inguérissables piqûres' (**142**).

Hitherto unconnected sensations may thus be brought together, often suggesting inner responses to external stimuli, as shown by the young Dominique, in his communion with nature at Les Trembles (**86**). Indeed, sense impressions can never be considered in isolation, since they need to be completed by the reaction produced on the pre-existing structure of the mind which receives them. If the mind is in a receptive state, an external stimulus is capable of becoming linked, by an elaborate pattern of correspondences, with everything that has previously been perceived or thought by that mind. The powers of memory can open up a vista of unexpected associations and all these complex activities are linked by tenuous threads to the operation of the imagination, which is thereby stimulated and set in motion. But what is the force which generates this complex process? Fromentin suggests that the impetus is due partly to the conscious willpower, 'la puissance de la volonté comme levier'. Its ultimate origin remains, however, a mystery, since the whole process is instituted and terminated by forces beyond human control.

To conclude, then, Dominique is not merely the self-projection of Fromentin: he is also the forerunner of the central figure in the *Künstlerroman*, the novel about novels, and its preoccupation with the growth of the artist.

Chapter Four

Landscape and seascape

When Fromentin started writing *Dominique*, in the autumn of 1859, he confided in Du Mesnil, saying: 'L'écueil c'est de n'être pas du *Gessner*, ni du *Berquin*, ni du *René*, ni mille choses' (3, p. 1171). Chateaubriand's *René* is well known to the public of today. The names of Salomon Gessner and Arnaud Berquin call, however, for a gloss: the former was a Swiss writer of pastorals; the latter, a writer of children's literature. That Fromentin should have felt the need to step out from their shadow is a clear indication that he was consciously writing in the tradition of the pastoral, more particularly in Chapter XI, the idyllic interlude at Les Trembles, which he himself described as 'cette courte pastorale' (**187**).

In *Fables of Identity*, Northrop Frye focused on analogy and identity as the two principles used by myth in assimilating nature to human form. This is more than the harmony between weather and human mood—of which there are many examples in *Dominique*: rain on the young hero's first day at school (**96**) and on his arrival in Paris (**152**); a sharp frost on the day of Madeleine's wedding (**141**) and on the day when the group left Les Trembles after their summer sojourn there (**187**). What Frye has in mind is, on the one hand, the 'parallels between human life and natural phenomena' (as in the cycle of the seasons and their assimilation to the human cycle of life, death and rebirth) and, on the other hand, 'the discrepancy between the world man lives in and the world he would like to live in' (64, p. 32).

The first of these, focusing on 'parallels between human life and natural phenomena', is echoed in the parallel between the return of the seasons and the cyclical structure of the novel. It is also implicit in the phrase for which the Swiss writer, Amiel, is famous: 'Un paysage, c'est un état d'âme', and of which Fromentin provides a textbook example, when Madeleine, at Les Trembles, remarks to Dominique: 'Votre pays vous ressemble':

> Je me serais doutée de ce qu'il était, rien qu'en vous voyant. Il est
> soucieux, paisible et d'une chaleur douce. La vie doit y être très calme
> et réfléchie. Et je m'explique maintenant beaucoup mieux certaines
> bizarreries de votre esprit, qui sont les vrais caractères de votre pays
> natal. (**176**)

Madeleine's real-life counterpart needed no introduction to these places,
where she and Fromentin grew up together. However, Fromentin invited
his new-found friend, Bataillard, to spend ten days with him in Saint-
Maurice, towards the end of the summer of 1840. It was like a rite of
passage. Just as Dominique would try to 'legitimise' his relationship with
Madeleine ('rendre notre amitié plus légitime') by establishing an analogy
between his identity and that of the nature in which he grew up ('mille
rapports d'éducation, d'intelligence, de sensibilité, presque de naissance et
de parenté' [**176**]), so, more than twenty years previously, Fromentin
had sought to initiate Bataillard into the whole secret of his childhood and
youth. He took him for walks in his garden, showed him the sea in all its
effects of light and shadow, as though he were taking him, 'page par page'
(3, p. 140), through the eighteen years of his life, more than half of which
flowed slowly through that little space. It is this ritual with Bataillard that
Fromentin is re-enacting fictionally, more than twenty years later, in
Chapter XI of *Dominique*. Indeed, just as the various characters were all
shown to have been cast in a composite self-portrait, so the landscape of
the novel is a self-projection of Fromentin. This is the most profoundly
autobiographical component in the book. Again to Bataillard, Fromentin
wrote, in 1842, saying that the whole story of his life was written at his
birth in his native region: 'c'est toujours ici qu'il faudra revenir pour en
trouver la clef, chaque fois que je me tromperai de direction et de but'. 'Je
me développe, vieillis et me fortifie pendant dix mois', he went on, 'puis
me rajeunis pendant les vacances' (p. 208). The concept of rejuvenation is
key here and leads to the second of Frye's principles.

     Year after year, returning to Saint-Maurice was an elixir of life for
Fromentin. It would soon take on the attributes of a dream place, an idyll,
in contrast to the imperfect world of everyday life. It will be remembered
that, when Fromentin outlined a haven of retreat to Du Mesnil, the
pinnacle of it all was to have been the possibility that he and his friends
might withdraw to Saint-Maurice. This dream rapidly took on the
attributes of a Golden Age, a world of fantasy, the fairytale world of

childhood. When Léocadie died in 1844 and was buried in the little cemetery of Saint-Maurice, all the memories associated with her were added to this growing metamorphosis of reality into art. In November 1844, Fromentin wrote to Bataillard, saying that he now found himself so far away from those serene, luminous times that, to him, they were 'mes temps fabuleux' (3, p. 311). Bergson believed that the 'fonction fabulatrice' was a human necessity, giving the mind instinctual images free from the perception of the empirical world or reason. It is in this sense that the pastoral at Les Trembles should be read. It poured forth from Fromentin, who wrote it and the long, descriptive introduction with scarcely a hesitation. Originally the idyll at Les Trembles was to precede the departure of Dominique and Madeleine to Paris and was to appear after Chapter VIII: by postponing it and thereby placing it in contrast with the anticlimax of Paris, Fromentin highlighted still further its magical power. Through pastoral, he was able to mask his identity and to allegorise his story, in the perception of the 'au-delà' (**180**) from the top of the lighthouse and in the timelessness of the boat scene, with the sea at dead calm (**180-3**).

Landscape is, thus, not just a setting, in Fromentin's novel: it functions in terms of pictorial metonymy. The hand of the *peintre-écrivain*, however, also makes itself felt, in Dominique's narration, when he tries out specific landscapes on Madeleine, to see what effect they would have on her. He talks about these landscapes in terms of 'tableaux' (**176**), composed by him, following the same reductive formula of basic horizontal coloured zones, signifying land, sky and sea. The effect is to bring the human percipient and the material environment together through a living dialogue, which simultaneously expresses the vigour of nature as a source of vibrant energy and the viewer's own actively aroused response. Every time Dominique succeeds in this, he sees it as a token of a 'nouvelle alliance' (**177**) between himself and Madeleine. At another level, it is just such an effect which Fromentin wants to arouse in his readers.

As a young man in Paris, he had sketched the environs of the city, in a manner reminiscent of the Dutch and English painters, as mediated through the influence of his mentor Louis Cabat, rather than in the

Italianate, neo-Classical style, advocated by his father. Classically trained
artists, for whom history painting still stood at the top of the hierarchy,
viewed landscape as a metaphor for a world in which human activity
predominates and in which nature provides merely a stage-like setting.
The young Fromentin's approach had much in common with that of the
Barbizon School, a movement which, as he himself noted (1, pp. 710-15),
was the visual counterpart, in the 1830s, of the first-generation Romantics
in literature. Like the Barbizon painters, Fromentin reduced the figure's
dominance over landscape and annotated his sketches, indicating the
precise location of each one of them, together with the date and, in some
cases, the hour of day—a visual counterpart of Dominique's memories as
a boy in the countryside around Villeneuve, remembering the local
weather conditions (**79**), or of his adult memories of the vacation at Les
Trembles, together with 'la date et le lieu précis de mille émotions bien
légères, et dont la trace est cependant restée' (**175**). Already, then,
Fromentin was using landscape images, in an iterative process, to observe
underlying patterns, an illustrated series anticipatory of those developed
later, on a far wider scale, by Monet, in his multiple views of Rouen
Cathedral. Universal truth, as encapsulated in neo-Classicism, was giving
way to relativism. Although the Impressionists were anathema to
Fromentin, from an art-historical point of view, it is interesting to note
that the highly visual memory of his eponymous hero, Dominique, is
characterised by its remarkable power of absorbing 'impressions' (**79**). As
Fromentin began to establish himself as a painter, he dropped the habit of
pinpointing the locations of his works, but signs of this practice are to be
found in his novel, where landscape and identity are closely integrated.

Of all the Barbizon painters, the one with whom Fromentin felt the
closest affinity was Théodore Rousseau. Many of the features of this
painter's art which he singles out for praise are characteristic of
Fromentin's own handling of landscape in *Dominique*. Describing him, in
Les Maîtres d'autrefois, as 'ce chercheur d'impressions nouvelles',
Fromentin highlights, in the work of Théodore Rousseau, 'cette étude du
relatif, de l'accidentel et du vrai' (1, p. 713). The ephemeral and the
contingent are key to his own presentation of the countryside around La
Rochelle. Portrayed as being without picturesque shapes, the ordinariness
and poverty of the countryside are deliberately brought out in a few tiny
touches at the beginning ('un grand pays plat [...,] nullement boisé, à peine

onduleux' [47]), leading up to the account of 'ce monotone et vaste paysage, dont l'indigence pittoresque eût paru complète sans la beauté singulière qui lui venait du climat, de l'heure et de la saison'. It is from the effect of changes in light, wind, warmth and movement that the delicate intensity of sensation will come, in an overall effect of synaesthesia. The sensations called up are not those aroused by descriptive detail and solid outline; they are sensations of space, dampness, shifting shades of light, sounds in the distance, slight scents. On the first walk through the night to Dominique's farm, for instance, the village through which the external narrator and the doctor pass is called up by just two sensations: the murmur of voices at supper behind closed shutters and the narrow ray of light passing through the keyholes, 'comme un trait rouge à travers la blancheur froide de la nuit' (49). The winepresses are open to the air and exude the moisture of crushed grapes, so that the hot exhalations of fermenting wine mingle with the smell of henhouses and stables. The wide stretch of the countryside is suggested by the crowing of cocks in the distance, which tells that the night will be damp. Migrant birds move and cry restlessly. Even the village festival is introduced with the sound of bagpipes, from far away across the plain. This night landscape is woven on the three sensations of moonlight, dampness and the distant music. Later, the main impression of the festival itself is of the servants moving back and forth across the courtyard with glimmering candles. When Dominique shows his visitors over the winepress, he does so in the half-light, as he moves with a lamp among the vacillating shadows, against a background of the warm, damp, heady odour of the wine. The sounds and movements of birds, the sense of space, the shifting and changing transparencies of light are constant themes in the landscape passages of *Dominique*. If Théodore Rousseau contributed to what Fromentin called *'l'école des sensations'* (1, p. 713), the same claim could be made for Fromentin himself in literature.

Sensations are used not only, of course, to evoke the countryside. When Dominique leaves his country home for Ormesson, it is through sensations that his apprehension and unhappiness are brought out: 'des brouillards fiévreux' and 'une humidité qui n'était plus celle de la mer' (93) set him shivering. When he arrives at the house of his aunt, Mme Ceyssac, the sense of being separated from his past and stifled by the rigid little provincial town is brought out less by analysis than by the vast, airless house and the smells of tar, hemp and pine planks hanging around the river port, just as later the smell of gaslight, amorphous pale faces and the changing sounds at night will call up Paris.

The sensations are not there simply in their own right, but as the means of suggesting the development and the essentials of feelings in characters. When he rushes back to his old home in the winter, the ice floating on the marshes in the darkness evokes his own desperate hurt until the old servant André, out shooting ducks, restores him to the rhythm of his own past. At the end, the 'tranquille horizon de plaine et d'eau' (**270**) is restored, framed by the window of the room in which Dominique had told his story. The oxen return after the day's ploughing, in a scene worthy of another Barbizon painter, Constantin Troyon. The oxen are part of the life of resignation and solid labour to which Dominique has returned. The warm rain of the dull day gives rise to a serene and golden evening, leading up, a little over-obviously, to the peaceful close of Dominique's story.

In Fromentin's milieu, as a boy and as a young adult, the paradigm for contemplative solitude in nature was hunting. Love and sympathy for the animals involved never extended so far as to criticise the hunt itself, as many people do today. For Fromentin, in particular, as for Dominique, 'la poursuite du gibier n'était que le prétexte d'un penchant plus vif, le désir de vivre au grand air et surtout le besoin d'y vivre seul' (**44**). Many of his North African paintings represented hunting scenes, showing the hunt as a noble activity, when practised with respect and restraint. Only once did he paint the quarry of the hunt—his most famous painting, *La Curée*, in 1863, the year after he completed *Dominique*—but even there, there is no sense of the animal's suffering. The portrait of the huntsman in Fromentin's novel is more in the style of the *Sketches of a Sportsman* (1847-1851) by Ivan Turgenev.

Significantly, it was M. de Nièvres who gave Dominique lessons in hunting. The men would go for long walks in the direction of the sea, shooting as they went, while the women followed them at a little distance or waited on the cliffs. Pictorially, Madeleine and Julie were like bright-coloured flowers among the pebbles at the edge of the blue sea. If they went too far afield, Madeleine's voice, calling them back, was borne on the wind, the sounds growing gradually fainter as they flew over 'ce pays sans écho' (**178**). Sometimes, as the sun went down, they would sit in contemplation, on the cliffs, watching the rollers that came from America dying at their feet. Like all peoples inhabiting the long corridor from the West African coast to Iceland and Greenland, they faced the ocean, which for so many centuries had represented the edge of the world, *Finis Terræ*, Land's End, a liminal place, neither of the land nor of the sea. Beyond the flashes of the lighthouses and the flares of some fishing vessels, the vast movement of the waters, heard but no longer seen across the darkness, lulled them into a silence in which each of them could pursue their own incommunicable reveries.

For one who did not greatly care for the sea, it is remarkable that one of Fromentin's most powerful scenes in the idyllic sojourn at Les Trembles should be a seascape. It is, however, a seascape with no storms, no action, no drama. On the contrary, it is high noon on a becalmed sea: a moment of perfect stasis, as Dominique and his visitors drift in the sun, 'ébloui de lumière, privés de conscience et pour ainsi dire frappés d'oubli' (**181**). This scene is markedly different from most visual narratives, which lead the eye from spot to spot, into a fictive space which underlies and produces traditional compositional coherence. The motionless sea is like a cauldron of half-melted lead. The sky is drained of colour by the dazzling noon-day light. The indeterminate space and limitless horizon produce an effect of emptiness and void, commonly now associated with abstract painting.

Even more so is this the case with the expedition to the lighthouse, which immediately precedes this seascape. Taking the typically Romantic trope of looking down from a lofty eminence, Fromentin marks himself out from his predecessors (Chateaubriand's René atop a volcano, Balzac's Rastignac challenging Paris from the heights of the Père-Lachaise cemetery, Stendhal's Fabrice experiencing his greatest happiness when in prison in a tower), by making his scene as flat and non-dramatic as the surrounding countryside. Situated at the end of a peninsula, in a small garden, hedged with tamarisks, this lighthouse is the highest vantage-point in the locality. Even from the base of the tower, the whole of the circular horizon is visible. As Dominique and his visitors go up the staircase, the roaring of the wind grows louder and growls like thunder as they ascend.

They emerge on to the platform of the lighthouse, to witness 'je ne sais quel murmure irrité dont rien ne peut donner l'idée quand on n'a pas écouté la mer de très haut' (**179**). Fromentin, whom Gautier later praised for being able to paint the wind by its effects (27), achieves a comparable result here, onomatopoeically, in the sentences which he inserted between 'Il faisait du vent' and 'Le ciel était couvert', in the manuscript version of his novel. As usual, with Fromentin, there is little analysis of what is going on in the mind—just one sentence, at the climax, on the sense of the fragility of life and the illusion of glimpsing something beyond. As they look out to the limitless horizon of the ocean, all the characters in the novel are awed. Madeleine gives a sort of anguished cry, as they lean in silence on the slight balustrade, which is all that separates them from the 'abîme' (**180**)—physically, the drop down a hundred feet and figuratively, the precipice of the forbidden, over which Madeleine and Dominique teeter perilously. Feeling the huge tower rocking under their feet at every impact of the wind and fascinated by an overwhelming sense of danger, the tension mounts. A string has to snap. It is Julie who nearly faints. She makes little of it, but the group goes down and the scene concludes.

The view from the top of the lighthouse is reminiscent of an Italian *veduta*. The reference to the platform of the lighthouse suggests also the viewing platform in the centre of a rotund panorama, from which a 360-degree view may be had, with no obstruction. In visual terms, the focalisation of Dominique on the lighthouse is quite different from that of René on Mount Etna. René, in his 'vue perpendiculaire du tableau', traces rivers like lines on a map and is almost vertiginously drawn to the crater of the volcano, but relates the entire scene to his own human predicament. Dominique's vision is one of the sea and the sky, in a double immensity, 'aussi haute qu'elle était profonde' (**179**). There is no vanishing point: only a keen eye could determine where the sea ends and the sky begins. The circular format devalues the individual viewpoint. The unfathomable Otherness of the external world is suggested in terms of sensory and cognitive dislocation, experienced differently by each member of the group. Rather than contributing to a build-up of personal identity, as in Chateaubriand's *René*, the focus turns to the crab-hunters in the rock-pools, the territory beyond the limits, where land and sea are in perpetual struggle and in relation to which all human endeavour is scaled down proportionately. The emptiness of the sea, as a 'bleu désert sans limites'

(**178**), combines with the abstract contemplation of the void, in a way which marks this scene out as one of the high points of Fromentin's suggestive art.

As a painter, Fromentin was well aware of the laws of linear perspective, drawn from geometry, and of the need to suggest the depth of three-dimensionality by means of tonal gradations in colour. These principles were developed, in fifteenth-century Florence, by Filippo Brunelleschi, Leon Battista Alberti and Paolo Uccello, whose famous remark to his wife is actually quoted in *Dominique*: '«Quelle douce chose que la perspective!»' (**242-3**). 'What is painting', Alberti had asked, in *De Pictura*, with reference to Narcissus, 'but the art of embracing [...] the surface of the pool?' Alberti then developed the idea of the 'open window', a fixed point through which the subject to be painted is seen, with the relative positions of the constituent parts being reconstructed spatially. By the nineteenth century, however, European landscape painting was beginning to break free from this 'window' tradition. In Caspar David Friedrich's *Monk by the Seaside* (1809-1810), thought to be a self-portrait of the artist, the spectator is viewed from the rear (a convention so popular in German Romantic painting that this type of figure became known as the *Rückfigur*), standing rooted on the shoreline and contemplating the infinite as an extension of his own inner universe. Constable, in his vast expanses of sea and sky, came close to dispensing with the horizon as a line of demarcation between two visually separate spheres. Turner, similarly, blended sky, sea and sand, in a way which was quite new. The fallibility and fragility of human perception was beginning to unsettle confidence in Albertian perspective.

Fromentin, in his own way, contributed to this shift in point of view. Dominique, as a boy, used to ride on a haywaggon, from which modest height he had a *constantly shifting* perspective on what *seemed* to be a limitless horizon. Beyond the green boundary line of the fields, the sea stretched as far as the eye could reach, giving rise to a sense of ecstasy, similar to that later experienced in the lighthouse scene: 'je ne sais quelle enivrante sensation d'un air plus large, d'une étendue plus vaste, me faisait perdre un moment la notion de la vie réelle' (**84**). The sea in question is not the Mediterranean, perceived as the basis of Western art ('une mer qui a vu des miracles, non pas divins, mais humains' [**210**]), but the Atlantic Ocean, perceived, by contrast, as the extreme of nothingness. In his study on Gustave Drouineau, Fromentin had criticised both Drouineau and Sainte-Beuve for identifying too closely with landscapes to which they could transfer their own emotions, in a style akin to that of the 'pathetic fallacy' adumbrated later by John Ruskin, in *Modern Painting* (1856):

> Les hommes trop intimes ne comprennent que le paysage intime, c.à.d. un paysage rétréci, le plus souvent mystérieux, dans lequel on peut aisément enfermer une idée ou un sentiment. —Ils le choisissent riant ou grave suivant la nature du sentiment ou de l'idée. —Les campagnes découvertes, les grands horizons de plaine ou de mer, les montagnes leur causent une impression confuse, les troublent, les fatiguent.—Ils se plaignent en leur présence d'une monotonie d'impressions qui vient précisément de leur inaptitude à les varier.—(2, p. 102)

Set alongside some notes made by Fromentin in preparation for a never-completed study of Sainte-Beuve, these remarks take on added significance:

> Analyse de nature. Il la voit de trop près [...].
> *Il la sent plus qu'il ne la voit*; trop de détails.
> Intimité jusque dans la description.
> Il ne voit dans la nature que son rapport psychologique avec un sentiment ou une idée. (1, p. 870)

Fromentin is here clearly distancing himself from his predecessors in several important ways. Firstly, mankind is no longer in centre-stage position, as in the 'anthropocentricity' implicit in Romanticism. Secondly, landscape encompasses, not merely features, but also emptiness—whether in relation to the desert or the sea. Having suggested the void of the Algerian desert in terms of that of the sea (1, p. 76), he subsequently suggested the void of the ocean by reference to the desert (**178**), rather than having recourse to direct representation. Thirdly, nature has to be seen as well as felt—which is where Fromentin's painterly talent conferred on him a position of privilege. For all these reasons, it is perhaps in his treatment of landscape and seascape that Fromentin is at his most original.

Chapter Five

Word and image

Fromentin told George Sand that *Dominique* contained the best part of him, his youth, which would never find a place in his pictures (3, p. 1233). Since his main claim to fame in painting was as an Orientalist, this remark is hardly surprising. In a deeper sense, however, it is only natural to look for a symbiosis of the textual and the visual in the work of one who was, as Sainte-Beuve put it, 'un peintre en deux langues' (51, p. 102). Yet Fromentin, in the preface which appeared at the head of the second edition of *Un été dans le Sahara* in 1874, insisted that he had at his disposal 'deux instruments distincts': 'le livre est là, non pour répéter l'œuvre du peintre, mais pour exprimer ce qu'elle ne dit pas' (1, p. 7). There was, he felt, no need for either medium to stray into the domain of the other. In particular, he distanced himself from the 'transposition d'art', as exemplified by Théophile Gautier, where the lines of demarcation between the different art forms became merged. Gautier, in his *Histoire du romantisme*, stressed the fruitful, reciprocal influences or borrowings between painting and literature, tracing them to the 1830s, but limiting himself to the abundance of colour vocabulary and references to art in Romantic writing. It is almost as though Fromentin, in his 1874 preface, sought to rebut the validity of this influence on the Parnassians by the Barbizon school of landscape, which led writers to enrich their vocabulary with colours drawn from the palette of painters (p. 6).

Painting confers the incalculable advantage of what Anthony Cronin, in one of his poems, describes as 'The calm, unassertive / Statement of paint / Without self-revelation' ('The Need of Words', in the collection *The Minotaur*). Self-revelation was anathema to Fromentin. He showed the draft of *Un été dans le Sahara* to his friend Du Mesnil, saying: 'Tu verras, s'il n'y pas trop *je*' (3, p. 968). So why was painting inadequate to give full expression to what Fromentin had to say? Because he wanted to project himself horizontally, through the various layers of his memory, rather than vertically, in a full-length portrait. Where painting is spatial and static, literature is temporal and sequential. Fromentin needed to write a fiction, in order to tell the truth. The process of writing enabled him to pass his memories through the prism of his creative imagination, structuring and designing the form of his evolving self-projection.

If words were needed, this was no problem to Fromentin. On 25 May 1865, the Goncourt brothers noted in their diary that he was one of the finest conversationalists on art and aesthetics whom they had ever heard (65: I, 166). By 'conversation', what is meant here is learned discourse, in the humanist tradition, characteristic of French *salons*, from the seventeenth century to the nineteenth century, where talking and writing were essentially two facets of the same activity. Indeed, in *Contre Sainte-Beuve*, Proust lashed out against what he perceived to be the superficiality of an approach to literature which is 'sur le même plan que la conversation'. The basic distinction, in this context, is between a literature which is oral in origin, born of social intercourse, and one which is hermetic and generated through extended monologue. The very qualities which Fromentin's father had thought would make him such a fine lawyer, balancing out the points at variance in any given argument, were those which were instilled in him by his training in rhetoric at school. His smallest missives obey the laws of classical balance and his full-blown letters are a marvel of polished writing. Antithesis makes itself felt, not merely in terms of the structure of *Dominique*, with Augustin and Olivier standing in polar opposition to each other, but even in the dialogue itself. 'Je ne puis empêcher ce qui est', Dominique says to Olivier, 'je ne puis prévoir ce qui doit être' (**162**). The Hamlet-like indecision of the protagonist is expressed as a balance of opposites: 'Ne plus aimer Madeleine ne m'est pas possible, l'aimer autrement ne m'est pas permis'. Augustin nearly talks in maxims. 'Beaucoup de gens', he pontificates, 'se lient pour éviter le mariage, qui devraient au contraire se marier pour briser des chaînes' (**220**). Olivier crystallises for Dominique the hopelessness of the situation in a telling antithesis: 'Essaye donc d'oublier Madeleine; moi, j'essayerai d'adorer Julie' (**232**). When, after the bouquet scene, the protagonist seeks to escape from himself and eschews Romantic fiction, he seeks to compile 'une sorte de recueil salutaire parmi ce que l'esprit humain a laissé de plus fortifiant, de plus pur au point de vue moral, de plus exemplaire en fait de raison' (**244**): this triad of elements is built up with a real sense of musical rhythm. At another level, the subtlety of definitions, for which Fromentin is justly famous, turns, not just on a multifaceted approach to abstract concepts, but also on a rhetorical love of balance. Does absence, for example, make the heart grow fonder? Or is it more a case of 'out of sight, out of mind'? Fromentin combines both positions in his pellucid statement: 'L'absence unit et désunit, elle rapproche aussi bien qu'elle divise, elle fait se souvenir, elle fait oublier' (54). Again, what is delightful, as a tie, is abominable if it becomes a chain (163). The whole question of sincerity, posed at various points throughout the novel and never directly answered, turns on the distinction made, at the outset, between resignation, which depends on ourselves, and oblivion, which only time can bring (42). Rhetoric, in other words, is the form which conditioned Fromentin's thinking; it is also an antiphonal dialogue between the living and the dead, between the present and the past, between the different voices brought to life through memory, personal and collective. It was his way of re-enacting his youth and all that was dearest to him in it.

At an early point in the novel, however, it becomes clear that words alone are not enough. '—Encore des regrets!' (52), said Dominique, in a tone which is described as 'plus significatif que les paroles', thereby arousing the curiosity of the external narrator. Dominique soon gave up writing (67; 70) and describes himself as 'un écrivain mécontent de lui qui renonce à la manie d'écrire' (76). He spoke of the countryside as a man who lives in it, never as a 'littérateur' (71)—itself a distinctly pejorative term. Olivier scorned writers (72). At the end of the idyllic stay at Les Trembles, Madeleine teased Dominique by identifying his problem with one of composing 'des rimes' (184). Indeed, there is a very negative image of writers throughout the novel. Penniless hacks, doomed to die of hunger, are described as writing away, in the reading-rooms of Paris libraries, with fever in their eyes, at books which would bring them neither wealth nor fame (158). The standing of writers is scarcely enhanced by the example of Augustin, with his mechanical method of drawing up lists of proper names, distinguishing them by some dominant characteristic and then arranging them, in varied combinations, as the *dramatis personæ* of a play. Even Augustin, however, seems to be endowed with some awareness of the oral origins of literature, since, as he wrote, clearly and fluently, he seemed to be dictating to himself in a whisper (87).

The problem, essentially, is the inadequacy of words themselves. They can have multiple meanings and can be ambiguous (140). Augustin sees that, for Dominique to be helped, he needs something more active and more efficacious than words, however sympathetic (**146**). For Fromentin, it is clear that one can write in more ways than just engage in penpushing, or what he calls the 'maniement de la plume' (**155**). For Dominique, a desk does not have to be made of wood: it can be a warm stone (**89**). Nor is a sheet of blank paper the only surface on which an inscription can be made; in the park at Les Trembles, the almond trees, bereft of leaves, hold up their fantastic tracery against the flaring skirts of the sunset (**82**). When the bunch of rhododendrons given to Madeleine is unwrapped, Olivier pounces on the visiting card, 'afin d'en examiner en quelque sorte la physionomie' (**125**). Despite the fact that there are few clear portraits in *Dominique* (as witness the 'visage indécis' of Mme de Bray [**53**]), pictorial awareness screams out from every page. In the park at Les Trembles, the square patches of colza dazzled the eye like blocks of gold (**84**). In Ormesson, the flying kites stood still against the clear blue sky, like white escutcheons picked out in bright colours (**106**). The huge sheaf of chrysanthemums held by Julie (**184**) heralds several treatments of that subject by later nineteenth-century painters. The complementary colours of red and green feature in the first family encounter in the novel (Mme de Bray's red scarf, set against the green path [**48**]), as also in nature, with autumn turning the trees red and the pastures green ('un groupe de grands chênes, les derniers à se dépouiller comme à verdir, qui gardaient leurs frondaisons roussâtres jusqu'en décembre' [**83**]). This last example is also indicative of Fromentin's concern to give nuance to his colour notations, in his use of the suffix '-âtre' to suggest 'reddish', 'blackish' (as in 'murs noirâtres' [**96**]) or 'whitish' (as in 'route blanchâtre' [**186**]).

Compositionally, *Dominique* presents like a succession of *tableaux,* many of them framed. When Madeleine returned from her vacation, the post chaise appeared, all white with dust, 'encadrée dans le rideau vert des charmilles' (**122**). Having stayed up all night talking to his former pupil, Augustin went over to the window to bathe his face in the icy morning air: his pale, angular features were outlined like a tragic mask on the field of the sky (**221**). Again, significantly, once the internal narrator has completed his *récit*, he looks towards the window, framing a peaceful horizon of open country and sea (**270**). Not merely are there a series of descriptive 'tableaux de la campagne' (**176**), but the action itself is propelled through visual resuscitation. The fateful marriage day of Madeleine is conveyed primarily through a 'tableau quasi imaginaire', with the phantasm of the bride—her flowers, her veil, her white gown—and the self-projection of Dominique's own youth, now dead: 'vierge, voilée et disparue' (**142**). At Les Trembles, when Dominique strove to order the memories of the idyllic interlude, he tried to compose a picture out of all that was best and least perishable in them (**184**). Later, when he imagines a possible scene in which he would confess to Madeleine his deep love for her, Dominique does so in terms of the 'tableau de mes douleurs' (**204**): in virtual reality, he pictures the reaction of Madeleine.

Metaphorical images abound in *Dominique*. The novel is, in many ways, a portrait of the artist as a huntsman, but it also shows the author identifying with the hunted animal. After the rupture with Madeleine, Dominique rushes back to Les Trembles, like a wounded animal losing blood and struggling to reach its hole before its strength gives out (**268**). The wounds of Augustin, sustained in his battle against adversity, are like the red stains that soak through the clothes of a wounded soldier (**170**). In Dominique's penultimate walk with Madeleine at Les Trembles, a thin clump of laurel separates the two and they walk in parallel, with the bushes between them (**184**). During the period when Madeleine is trying to 'cure' Dominique of his love for her, she is portrayed, in an image reminiscent of Sainte-Beuve's *Volupté*, as being as calm as the surface of a sheltered lake (**216**). On the shores of the Mediterranean, Dominique, conscious of both the finite and the infinite in man, watches a white bird flying, the slender span of its spread wings outlined against the changeless blue of the sky and mirrored in the level sea (**210**).

What is common to all these images is the extent to which they seek to combine the pictorial and the non-visual. Sainte-Beuve was the first of many critics to detect this procedure in Fromentin's description of 'un ciel balayé, brouillé, soucieux' (1, p. 40). The use of an abstract epithet to qualify a concrete substantive, as in this example of 'un ciel [...] soucieux', represents the blending of the outer world of nature with the inner world of the artist, or what Sainte-Beuve described as 'cette fusion du moral dans le naturel' (51, p. 111), where 'moral' means 'non-physical' rather than 'ethical'. This procedure, well described by Victor Waille as the transmutation of 'un mot usuel et terne' into 'un mot presque phosphorescent' (56, p. 320), is clearly exemplified in the description of the sadness and monotony of Ormesson in terms of its 'silence hargneux' (**98**). When Dominique visits Madeleine's room in her absence, he is struck by the 'étoffes de couleur sobre' and the 'blancheur de l'effet [...] le plus recueilli' (**115-16**). By means of this skilful interweaving of the vague and the precise, he succeeds in evoking those subjective impressions which so often perpetuate an experience in the memory. From this point of view, it is significant that most of Fromentin's work was composed in retrospect, since, by writing from memory, he claimed that he could achieve a balance vital to his art, between precision and abstraction: precision, as recorded by his remarkably acute memory; abstraction, as evolved through the passage of time. The experiences thus described are neither wholly imaginary nor wholly factual. They combine something of both these qualities in an aesthetic form which, in Fromentin's own words, is 'moitié réelle et moitié imaginaire' (1, p. 295).

By means of this technique, centred on a delicate Verlaine-like balance, 'où l'Indécis au Précis se joint', Fromentin sought above all to evoke subjective reactions. When he was describing the desert, for example, he was reluctant to use yellow, the colour normally associated with sand. Instead, he described it in all the ways in which it appeared to him and insisted that it was for each individual to express it for themselves. They should, he said, 'en fixer le ton d'après la préférence de leur esprit' (1, p. 30). In seeking to engage the participation of the reader in the recreation of experiences, Fromentin's technique comes close at times to that adopted by the Goncourt brothers, especially in relation to the procedure commonly known as 'nominal syntax' and described with particular clarity by Stephen Ullmann, in *Style in the French Novel* (71). This procedure involves the use a noun where normal usage might have dictated an adjective or a verb; the noun, as a result, usurps the dominant position in the sentence and is made to suggest the desired impression.

Taking, first of all, the merging of adjectives into nouns, in the work of Fromentin, this technique involves the transference of an adjective from its position of secondary importance following the object which it qualifies, to the position of an abstract quality-noun dominating the phrase in which it appears. Thus, where one might have expected to find 'une statue blanche et inanimée', Fromentin instead has 'la blancheur inanimée d'une statue' (**252**).

The full effect of this device may be seen by placing this fragment in its context. Dominique, having voluntarily exiled himself for some time from the world of Madeleine, suddenly returns to Nièvres, on hearing that Julie is ill. In describing this return, Fromentin has faithfully retained the sequence of impressions in the exact order in which Dominique might have experienced them: getting down from the post-chaise in the dark, seeing first of all a blaze of lights and only identifying them afterwards, meeting someone in the half-darkness of the hall and not realising immediately that it was Madeleine herself. Even at this stage, the dominant impression experienced by the protagonist was one of whiteness, with Madeleine enveloped in 'la blancheur inanimée d'une statue'. Only gradually did his eye come to rest on her physical attributes, as she clasped his hand. Fromentin's technique here is admirably suited to the suggestive effect of the passage, for two reasons. Firstly, the gradual unfolding of these impressions is a faithful reproduction of the order in which they would normally be experienced and reflects a procedure vital to any form of art which seeks to enlist not merely the sympathy but also the collaboration of the percipient. Secondly, the quality is detached from the person or object which it describes and is given an independent existence—a technique which is an exact literary equivalent of the parallel device in Impressionist painting, whereby colour takes precedence over form. In both cases, the impressions are preserved with the utmost fidelity, from their first impact on the retina of the eye to their ultimate cerebral interpretation.

The merging of verbs into nouns, equally a part of Fromentin's nominal syntax, takes the form of weakening the verb as much as possible and concentrating the main effect of the sentence into an abstract noun. In this way, it is possible to capture the most fleeting impressions, without interrupting their flow by the intrusion of any finite action. Thus, in describing Dominique's final return to Les Trembles, instead of 'des souvenirs tressaillirent en moi', Fromentin has 'il y eut en moi un tressaillement de souvenirs' (**268**), a device by which the essentially passive nature of the experience can be more effectively conveyed. This technique, whereby action-nouns can be introduced by 'avoir', has the advantage of enabling them to be used in the plural and, as a result, is particularly valuable in conveying lingering impressions. The description of the Seine begins: 'La rivière avait des frissons de lumière qui la blanchissaient' (**240**). The use of the plural here conveys an effect of prolonged shimmering in the moonshine and provides an admirable setting for the touch of colour contained in the final verb. That this was a technique consciously adopted by Fromentin is evident from the fact that, in relation to the initial description of Madeleine, where the manuscript contained a reference, in mid-sentence, to 'la blancheur de ses joues' (4, p. 350), the definitive version foregrounds the dominant impression of paleness, suggestive of repressed convent life, by placing the single adjective, 'blanche', at the beginning of the sentence: 'Blanche, elle avait des froideurs de teint qui sentaient la vie à l'ombre et l'absence totale d'émotions' (**100**). The impression thus created is quickly consolidated by the abstract quality-noun 'froideurs', used in the plural with 'avoir', to convey the idea of duration.

The question of Fromentin's position in relation to Impressionism is one which requires some comment. Having been adventurous in his youth, Fromentin, as a painter, became increasingly conservative. A member of the all-powerful *jury*, which sat in judgement on the submissions for the annual *Salon* exhibition, he was deeply hostile to those painters who, after 1874, came to be known as the Impressionists. What troubled him mostly about their work was its lack of finish, whereas he had been brought up to believe that a world of difference separated the study from the final painting. He felt so strongly on the subject that his major motivation, in going to Belgium and the Netherlands in 1875, was to show these young painters the errors of their ways and to remind them of the lessons of the Old Masters. What he found there did not always accord with his expectations. Fundamentally, however, and long before the last decade of his life, Fromentin had been attracted by many of the features characteristic of Impressionism, in its visual and verbal forms. The examples of nominal syntax have already shown the extent of Fromentin's concern with the *effects* on the reader of what he is describing. The external narrator seeks to recreate for the reader the 'voies indirectes' (**65**), by which he himself followed the progression from the commonplace life of the gentleman farmer to the very consciousness of the man. When the internal narrator wants to convey something of the morbid sensibility of the young Dominique, he introduces the anecdote concerning the essay on Hannibal at Zama with the remark: 'Un seul détail vous en donnera l'idée' (**89**). Visually, the light winter mist in the park at Les Trembles put blue into its depths and made all distances deceptive (**86**). The prizegiving scene gives a word picture, with light, vaporous touches, of subjects such as the Impressionist painters were later to express on canvas, in works like Monet's *Femmes au jardin* (1867): Madeleine coming with a group of young women, their trailing skirts raising a fine dust which followed them like a light cloud; blossoms falling from the yellowing branches and settling on Madeleine's long, muslin scarf; the ladies' open parasols chequered with sunshine and shadow (**149**).

———

Though Fromentin never deviates from his belief in the generic specificity of the arts, there is a strong case for considering *Dominique* as a visual novel, on the grounds of pictorial awareness—ranging from the tiniest colour notation to the imagistic composition of scenes as *tableaux*—and also because of its emphasis on perception as the principal mode of interaction among the fictional characters. The number of references to the natural eye is striking. As a boy, in winter, Dominique's eyes lost none of their keenness as they learned to pierce the December fogs and the vast curtains of rain (**86**). Eyes are either half-closed (in the case of Julie, on the point of fainting, in the lighthouse scene [**180**]) or wide open (when Madeleine met Dominique unexpectedly in Nièvres: 'elle [...] ouvrit démesurément des yeux égarés' [**253**]). In Paris, Augustin's eyes were wider open and brighter (**155**). Even the banal phrase, 'with open eyes', has greater force than usual, in this novel, where communication is essentially visual. With hindsight, Dominique admits that the gift of the rhodendrons ought to have opened his eyes (**124**). Later, as he came to understand the impossibility of the situation between Julie and Olivier, a number of incidents finally opened his eyes (**229**). Exasperated, Olivier remarks: 'Julie a des yeux qui me trouveraient là où je ne suis pas' (**226**). Suspension of reason is equated with blindness (**125**). Mirrors can give an added dimension to communication, as when Dominique broke with a mistress, who then met his eyes in her looking glass (**174**). Ocular instruments, such as opera glasses, reinforce the thematic role of vision, as when two unescorted women, associated with what Dominique calls his 'anciennes faiblesses', 'commencèrent à lorgner, et leurs yeux s'arrêtèrent sur la loge de Madeleine' (**238**): their determined gaze provoked the jealousy of the heroine and led to her biting her bouquet and tearing it to pieces. Looks most definitely count in this novel.

Looks and looking. Though seemingly an intermediary, the visual medium affords a more direct communication, because it supplants conventional verbal structures with its own visual language and sign system. It follows that 'le regard' has a major functional role in *Dominique*. For more than eighteen months, the protagonist had 'watched', but had never 'seen', Madeleine. When he did, it was a revelation: 'je venais de la regarder comme on regarde quand on veut voir' (**113**). The realisation that Madeleine was betrothed came to Dominique as he stood on a stone seat outside and looked in the window at a scene in which the whole family seemed to be re-enacting Greuze's celebrated picture *L'Accordée de village*: 'personne ne pouvait se douter que j'étais là; je plongeai les yeux dans le salon' (**135**). Julie sat motionless, her wide-open eyes fixed on the stranger, M. de Nièvres. Later, when all were present, Madeleine indicated her acceptance of him as her future husband by 'un rapide regard' (**139**) around the room. The principal features of Julie are her sphinx-like appearance, her look ('regard' [**141**]), which sometimes asked questions but never answered any, and eyes that drank everything in. As Dominique stood on the platform, after being awarded his school prize, the first eyes to meet his, together with his aunt's, were Madeleine's (**150**). When he burned his early writing and Olivier returned to find the heap of smoking ashes, no verbal explanation was needed: a quick glance said it all (**161**). In the ball scene, seeing is linked with sexuality, when Madeleine appeared to Dominique for the first time in all the revealing splendour of evening dress. Instead of returning her 'regard paisible' (**188**), he stared awkwardly at a cluster of diamonds, sparkling on her breast. She blushed a little, shivered—as if she suddenly felt cold—and wrapped a lace scarf round her shoulders. Afterwards, she looked at him two or three times, for no apparent reason, as though she had had a surprise which she could not get over, but the wordless drama of the situation is conveyed entirely through the characters' examination of each other.

The act of watching is so central to *Dominique* that, in this novel, voyeurism becomes the ultimate symbol of sexual desire and possession. Dominique is a *voyeur* in Madeleine's bedroom when she is away (**115-16**), at her engagement (**135**), and as he watches her asleep on the boat, her limp hands fallen, just open, beside her husband's, and her lips slightly parted (**182**). She is, for him, a mental image—partly remembered, but mostly composed. Indeed, such are his inhibitions that he lives much of his early life as a *voyeur*. He went to the theatre one night, for no other reason than to watch Olivier (**172-3**). After publishing two volumes anonymously, he then summed himself up in two books which appeared under a pseudonym: he took a delicate relish in the strictly private pleasure of hearing himself praised in the person of his alias (**245**). It is as though the taboo areas of Dominique's consciousness are fetishised and can only be accessed visually.

So Dominique's love for Madeleine is impossible for reasons which far transcend the bounds of societal convention. She is an untouchable icon, who can only be conjured up in the paradoxical state of being 'present in absence': the mental images of her meld, in Fromentin's creative imagination, while his use of words preserves the necessary distance for the illusion to be maintained. It is on that basis that the novel develops until Chapter XVI, when this entire procedure is reversed. Here, Madeleine is not immediately fetishised into an icon. On the contrary, her image comes to life in her portrait, displayed in a public gallery. This crucial scene must have been written at a late stage in the composition of the novel, since there is no trace of it in the manuscript. It has been said that it was yet another example of Fromentin plundering the arsenal of well-worn scenes to flesh out the action of his novel. There was, of course, the precedent (among others) of *La Princesse de Clèves*, where the heroine's miniature portrait is stolen by the duc de Nemours and is subsequently missed by her husband, who remarks—at this point in the novel, without conviction—that it must have been removed by some secret lover. Here, the portrait, as object, serves a key role in the plot, something like the handkerchief in *Othello*. What differentiates the portrait scene in *Dominique* is that the image of Madeleine is resuscitated in 'ce fantastique entretien d'un homme vivant et d'une peinture' (**251**). Dominique, of course, is still the *voyeur*. Day after day, he returned to the gallery, pushing his way past the tiresome *amateurs* coming between him and the portrait. So as not to draw attention to himself, he pretended to be a knowledgeable expert and behaved as though he were passionately interested in the artist's work, whereas all his passion was in his adoration of the model. Madeleine was gazing at him—'mais avec quels yeux!' (**250**) She seemed mysterious in her look of expectancy and of bitter reproach. When Dominique stood before the picture, it ceased to be a work of art: 'c'était Madeleine de plus en plus triste'. In 1867, Zola had the eyes of the portrait of Camille (the murdered first husband of Thérèse Raquin, painted by Laurent, her second husband and author of the crime plotted by both of them) haunt the couple, in a hallucinated form, on their wedding night: hearing a sound, Laurent was afraid that Camille was going to step out of the picture; later, he felt incapable of ever painting any figure other than that of Camille. However, it would not be until 1890 that Oscar Wilde, in *The Picture of Dorian Gray*, would grant his protagonist's mad wish that he himself might remain young and his portrait grow old, thus taking still further the catalytic role played by a painting, 'with a life of its own'. Already in *Dominique*, however, the portrait plays a pivotal role in the development of the plot. It enables Madeleine to step out of the frame, so to speak, and engage with the protagonist. After the shock of seeing Dominique unexpectedly in Nièvres, when she was petrified with surprise and as white as a statue, Madeleine reappeared, five minutes later, dressed in dark colours and looking exactly like the portrait, 'avec la vie de plus' (**254**). Dominique's inhibitions are exorcised sufficiently for him to be able to speak to her, touch her and kiss her. It is the portrait which brought about this metamorphosis: the gleam in her eyes combined with the indefinable drawing of her mouth to give this 'muette effigie' (**251**) a frightening mobility. Madeleine's visible anguish emboldened Dominique at Nièvres. He embraced her, she confessed her love for him, she became 'accessible'—unlike the princesse de Clèves before her or Mme Arnoux (of Flaubert's *L'Éducation sentimentale*) after. Dominique and Madeleine chose to go their separate ways, for all the reasons which have been indicated already. To these may now be added Fromentin's desire to preserve the mental image of his love, in a private cocoon, spun from the visual and the verbal elements of his creative imagination.

Conclusion

Dominique is the single novel of a *peintre-écrivain*. Yet it has many resonances in the creative inner world of Fromentin. It can be seen to contain multiple self-projections of its author, not merely in the person of the eponymous hero, but also in that of the heroine, Madeleine, in the hero's study and the natural landscape which forms the catalyst and complement of the human emotions suggested. Like a theme with variations, the lived experience of Fromentin and Léocadie Chessé was repeated, first in the novel and subsequently in the re-enactment of both life and art, in Fromentin's crafted monologues, addressed to Hortense Howland, the object of his Platonic devotion. In the novel, he places this theme in the age-old context of man's dread of being caught in the toils of a *femme fatale* (as underscored in Constant's *Adolphe*), in a way which suggests a basic fear of femininity and a retreat to the safe haven of the androgyne (as characterised on a more grandiose scale in the work of Fromentin's friend and fellow-painter, Gustave Moreau). Barthes suggests that the anguished cry, '«Madeleine est perdue, et je l'aime!»' (**136**) should read: 'J'aime Madeleine parce qu'elle est perdue' (16, p. 166), in conformity with the Orphic myth whereby loss defines love. A Freudian analysis of the novel might expand on the absence of paternal and maternal figures in the metamorphosis of the author's youth, from a world in which his own father was dominant and his mother almost stiflingly close, to one in which the characters were virtually *sans famille*.

Echoes of Ovid's *Metamorphoses* make themselves felt throughout in the abyss separating the real and the ideal, in which the ambivalence of human sentiment is paramount and the duality of human personality ever-present. The final ride on horseback by Dominique and Madeleine is reminiscent of Fromentin's pictures of Arab falconers, galloping towards the ideal, towards the impossible. Yet this *perpetuum mobile* is inexorably coupled with its opposite—a love of all that is static: 'J'aime peu ce qui court, ce qui coule, ou ce qui vole', he wrote in 1844, 'toute chose immobile, toute eau stagnante, tout oiseau planant ou perché, me cause une indéfinissable émotion' (3, p. 312). In his paintings, as in his writings, Fromentin focuses on the sequels to action rather than on action itself. His evocation of femininity is contemplative, seen at a distance, *figée*—

anticipatory, in some ways, of Georges Rodenbach's *Bruges-la-Morte*. A painter in two media, he nevertheless suggests more than he shows and evokes the world of dreams and myths, rather than the world of reality.

Metamorphosis is central to the threefold process whereby Fromentin takes the physical sense impressions of lived experience, passes them through the crucible of memory and the creative imagination, and transforms them into art. They then take on a quite 'other' existence, in which silence is often more eloquent than words. And so *Dominique*, which, from certain points of view, may appear anachronistic, can, in another light, be seen as modern, by virtue of its non-finality, its suggestivity and its self-reflexivity. It constitutes a landmark, in the history of the confessional novel, in function of the non-teleological nature of its narrative. In the words of Jean Bessière, it is 'une reprise de René' and a 'contre-René' (9, p. 238). Or, as Bernard Pingaud has put it, Fromentin, in writing this work, sought not merely to prove himself a novelist: 'il se propose aussi de montrer la faillite du romanesque' (6, p. 25). Dominique ends, as the external narrator tells us at the outset, by wanting a self-effacement that lets him blend into the mass of '*quantités négatives*' (**42**) in society: from eponymous he wills himself to become anonymous.

This marks a shift away from the anthropocentric universe, which has a clear parallel in the foregrounding of landscape as a force in its own right, recognised as an entity lying outside humanity, yet capable of generating affective responses. With this comes a greater emphasis on the visual and a concomitant distrust of the power of words. Crippled by timidity, Dominique is inarticulate in a crisis. Human communication between the characters in the novel is by *regards*. At one level, Dominique may be seen as silently burying himself alive; and Olivier—whose own fate so mirrors his—writes, after his attempted suicide: 'C'est bien véritablement un mort qui t'écrit' (**75**). Madeleine, who, throughout the novel, is a mental image in Dominique's consciousness, present in absence, comes to life through her representation in a painting. The novel progresses from *tableau* to *tableau*, as a series of silent visual encounters, termed 'dumb shows' by Richard Bales (15, p. 129). 'Words have been my only loves, not many', wrote Samuel Beckett in *From an Abandoned Work*. There were images too, as Beckett well knew. Perhaps it was necessary to await the twentieth-century rekindling of interest in interdisciplinarity for the seamless continuity of word and image in Fromentin to be fully appreciated.

Select bibliography

Paris is the place of publication of works published in France,
except where otherwise indicated.

Editions of works by Fromentin

1. *Œuvres complètes,* ed. Guy Sagnes, NRF Gallimard, 'Bibliothèque de la Pléiade', 1984.

2. *Gustave Drouineau* [with Émile Beltremieux], ed. Barbara Wright, Minard, 'Archives des lettres modernes', 97, 1969 [1842].

Correspondence

3. *Correspondance d'Eugène Fromentin*, ed. Barbara Wright, Paris / Oxford: CNRS-Éditions / Universitas, 2 vols., 1995.

Editions of *Dominique*

4. Librairie Marcel Didier, Société des textes français modernes, ed. Barbara Wright, 2 vols., 1965.

5. Garnier-Flammarion, GF 141, ed. Guy Sagnes, 1967.

6. Gallimard, 'Folio', 644, ed. Bernard Pingaud and S. de Sacy, 1974.

7. Garnier-Flammarion, GF 479, ed. Pierre Barbéris, 1987.

8. Éditions de l'Imprimerie nationale, ed. Anne-Marie Christin, 1988.

9. Larousse, ed. Jean Bessière, 1989.

10. Le Livre de Poche, 'Classiques de Poche', ed. Philippe Dufour, 2001.

Bibliography

11. Wright, Barbara, *Eugène Fromentin: A Bibliography*, London: Grant and Cutler, Research Bibliographies and Checklists, 1973; supplement no. 1, 1998.

General studies of Fromentin

12. Thompson, James and Barbara Wright, *La Vie et l'œuvre d'Eugène Fromentin*, ACR, 1987.

13. Wright, Barbara, *Eugène Fromentin: A Life in Art and Letters*, Bern: Lang, 2000.

Specialised studies of *Dominique*

14. Arland, Marcel, '*Dominique* et Fromentin', in *Les Échanges* (Gallimard, 1946), pp. 205-29.

15. Bales, Richard, 'Strategies of Persuasion in Fromentin's *Dominique*', in *Persuasion in the French Personal Novel* (Birmingham, AL: Summa Publications, 1997), pp. 113-39.

16. Barthes, Roland, 'Fromentin: *Dominique*', in *Le Degré zéro de l'écriture*, suivi de *Nouveaux Essais critiques* (Seuil: 1972), pp. 156-69.

17. Blanche, Jacques-Émile, *Hommage à André Gide* (Éditions du Capitole, 1928), p. 102.

18. Brahimi, Denise, 'Fromentin: *Dominique*', in *Charmes de paysage* (Saint-Cyr-sur-Loire: Christian Pirot, 1994), pp. 72-84.

19. Chadourne, Louis, *L'Inquiète Adolescence* (Albin Michel, 1920), p. 139.

20. Cressot, Marcel, 'Le Sens de *Dominique*', *Revue d'histoire littéraire de la France*, XXXV, 2 (avril-juin 1928), 211-18.

21. Daudet, Léon, 'Les Faux Chefs-d'œuvre, II: À propos de *Dominique*', in *Écrivains et artistes* (Éditions du Capitole, 1928), pp. 215-24.

22. Delancre, Pierre, '*Dominique* ou la cohérence en creux', *Revue des sciences humaines*, XXXVI, 143 (juillet-septembre 1971), 373-80.

23. Dorbec, Prosper, 'La Sensibilité de l'artiste dans *Dominique*', *Revue bleue* (6 novembre 1920), 645-9.

24. Favre, Yves-Alain, 'Fromentin et le paysage intérieur dans *Dominique*', in *Ouest et Romantismes*, ed. Georges Cesbron (Presses de l'Université d'Angers, 1991), pp. 297-303.

25. Fleming, John A., 'Representational A, B, Cs: Cipher and Structure in *Dominique*', *Romanic Review*, 77, 2 (March 1986), 116-24.

26. Garcin, Philippe, 'Le Souvenir dans *Dominique*', *Nouvelle Revue française* (1 janvier 1957), pp. 111-21; repr. in *Partis-pris* (Payot, 1977), pp. 168-77.

27. Gautier, Théophile, 'Salon de 1859', VI, *Le Moniteur universel*, 28 mai 1859.

28. Gide, André, 'Les Dix Romans français que...', *La Nouvelle Revue française*, 52 (avril 1913), 533-41 [pp. 538-9], reprinted in *Incidences* (Gallimard, 1924), pp. 149-56 [p. 154].

29. Gillet, Louis, 'Eugène Fromentin et *Dominique*, d'après des documents inédits', *Revue de Paris* (1er août 1905), 526-58.

30. Gougenheim, Georges, 'La Présentation du discours indirect dans *La Princesse de Clèves* et dans *Dominique*', *Le Français moderne*, VI, 4 (octobre 1938), 305-20 [reprinted 1970].

31. Greshoff, C.J., 'Fromentin's *Dominique*', in *Seven Studies in the French Novel, from Mme de La Fayette to Robbe-Grillet* (Cape Town: A.A. Balkema, 1964 [1961]), pp. 53-70.

32. Grimsley, Ronald, 'Romanticism in *Dominique*', *French Studies*, XII, 1 (January 1958), 44-57.

33. Harris, Trevor, *'Dominique' ou la géométrie de la mauvaise conscience*, University of Salford, Working Papers in Literature and Cultural Studies, December 1992.

34. Herzfeld, Claude, *'Dominique' de Fromentin: thèmes et structure*, Nizet, 1977.

35. Herzfeld, Claude, 'L'Aunis imaginaire de Fromentin', in *Ouest et Romantismes*, ed. Georges Cesbron (Presses de l'Université d'Angers, 1991), pp. 305-15.

36. Larthomas, Pierre, 'Écriture romanesque et écriture poétique: le *Dominique* de Fromentin', in *Études de lexicologie, lexicographie et stylistique offertes en hommage à Georges Matoré*, ed. Irène Tamba (Université de Paris-IV [Sorbonne], 1987), pp. 5-17.

37. Lehtonen, Maija, 'Essai sur *Dominique* de Fromentin', *Annales Academiæ Scientiarum Fennicæ*, Ser. B., CLXXVI (Helsinki: Suomalainen Tiedeakatemia, 1972).

38. Lethbridge, Robert, 'Fromentin's *Dominique* and the Art of Reflection', *Essays in French Literature*, XVI (November 1979), 43-61.

39. Magowan, Robin, 'Fromentin', in *Narcissus and Orpheus: Pastoral in Sand, Fromentin, Jewett, Alain-Fournier and Dinesen* (New York / London: Garland, 1988), pp. 38-67.

40. Martin, Graham Dunstan, 'The Ambiguity of Fromentin's *Dominique*', *The Modern Language Review*, 77, 1 (January 1982), 38-50.

41. Massis, Henri, '*Dominique* ou la confession inutile', in *Jugements* (Plon, 1924), pp. 283-92.

42. Mavrakis, Annie, 'Décrire l'invisible: sur *Dominique* de Fromentin', *Poétique*, 100 (novembre 1994), 435-47.

43. Mein, Margaret, 'Fromentin: A Precursor of Proust', in *A Foretaste of Proust* (Farnborough, Hants: Saxon House, 1974 [1971]), pp. 8. 9; 39; 76; 143-60; 186-7.

44. Monge, Jacques, 'Un précurseur de Proust: Fromentin et la mémoire affective', *Revue d'histoire littéraire de la France*, LXI, 4 (oct.-déc. 1961), 564-88.

45. Reynaud, Camille, *La Genèse de 'Dominique'*, Grenoble: Arthaud, 1937.

46. Richard, Jean-Pierre, 'Paysages de Fromentin', in *Littérature et sensation* (Seuil, 1954), pp. 221-62.

47. Rinsler, Norma, 'Fromentin's *Dominique*', in *Studies in French Fiction in Honour of Vivienne Mylne*, ed. Robert Gibson (London: Grant and Cutler, 1988), pp. 243-61.

48. *Romantisme*, 23 (1979), 99-121. '*Dominique*, la fin du romantisme' (publications emanating from a seminar on Dominique held at the École normale supérieure de Saint-Cloud and, later, at the Université de Caen between 1975 and 1978).

49. Rosen, Elisheva, *Dénégation et figurabilité dans 'Dominique' de Fromentin*, Université de Paris-VIII doctoral thesis, 1978.

50. Sagnes, Guy, 'Les Formes du regard dans *Dominique*', in *Colloque Eugène Fromentin*, ed. Pierre Golliet, Travaux et mémoires de la Maison Descartes, no. 1 (Amsterdam / Lille: Publications de Lille-III, 1979), pp. 98-111.

51. Sainte-Beuve, Charles-Augustin, '*Dominique*', in *Nouveaux Lundis*, VII (Michel Lévy, 1867), 127-50.

52. Thibaudet, Albert, 'Fromentin', in *Intérieurs* (Plon, 1924), pp. 149-90.

53. Traz, Robert de, '*Dominique* ou l'honneur bourgeois', *Esprits nouveaux* (août-septembre 1922); repr. in *Essais et analyses* (Crès, 1926), pp. 145-66.

54. Tritsmans, Bruno, 'D'une écriture mineure: contrainte et invention dans *Dominique* d'Eugène Fromentin', *Versants*, 17 (1990), 85-101.

55. Vier, Jacques, *Pour l'étude du 'Dominique' de Fromentin*, Minard, 'Archives des lettres modernes', 16-17, 1958.

56. Waille, Victor, 'Le Monument de Fromentin', *Revue africaine* (1903), 312-34.

57. Wright, Barbara, 'Fromentin's Concept of Creative Vision in the Manuscript of *Dominique*', *French Studies*, XVIII, 3 (July 1964), 213-26.

58. Wright, Barbara, '*Valdieu*: A Forgotten Precursor of Fromentin's *Dominique*', *The Modern Language Review*, LX, 4 (October 1965), 520-8.

59. Wright, Barbara, 'L'Édition des *Reliquiæ* de Gustave Millot par Paul Bataillard: un avatar inconnu du *Dominique* de Fromentin', *Australian Journal of French Studies*, XXIV, 2 (1987), 165-74.

60. Wright, Barbara, 'L'Image du chasseur dans *Dominique* et sa genèse dans l'œuvre picturale d'Eugène Fromentin', in *L'Image génératrice des textes de fiction*, ed. Pascaline Mourier-Casile et Dominique Moncond'huy (Poitiers: La Licorne, 1996), pp. 99-104.

General works

61. Abrams, Meyer Howard, *Natural Supernaturalism: Tradition and Revolution in Romantic Literature*, New York: Norton, 1971.

62. Brunetière, Ferdinand, 'La Littérature personnelle', in *Questions de littérature*, Calmann-Lévy, 1897.

63. Corbin, Alain, 'Coulisses', in *De la Révolution à la Grande Guerre, 4, Histoire de la vie privée*, ed. Michelle Perrot, Seuil, 1987.

64. Frye, Northrop, 'Myth, Fiction and Displacement', in *Fables of Identity*, New York: Harcourt Brace Jovanovich, 1951.

65. Goncourt, Edmond and Jules de, *Journal. Mémoires de la vie littéraire*, ed. Robert Ricatte, Laffont, 'Bouquins', 3 vols., 1989 [1956].

66. Hytier, Jean, *Les Romans de l'individu*, Les Arts et le Livre, 1928.

67. Lejeune, Philippe, *Le Pacte autobiographique*, Seuil, 1975.

68. Merlant, Joachim, *Le Roman personnel, de Rousseau à Fromentin*, Hachette, 1905.

69. O'Brien, Justin, *The Novel of Adolescence in France*, New York: Columbia University Press, 1937.

70. Sheringham, Michael, *French Autobiography: Devices and Desires*, Oxford: Clarendon Press, 1993.

71. Ullmann, Stephen, 'New Patterns of Sentence-Structure in the Goncourts', in *Style in the French Novel* (Cambridge University Press, 1957), pp. 121-45.